The Objec[...]
to magic: [...]
and animate them with a rich history of invention,
political struggle, science, and popular mythology.
Filled with fascinating details and conveyed in sharp,
accessible prose, the books make the everyday world
come to life. Be warned: once you've read a few of these,
you'll start walking around your house, picking up
random objects, and musing aloud: 'I wonder what the
story is behind this thing?'"

Steven Johnson, author of *Where Good Ideas
Come From* and *How We Got to Now*

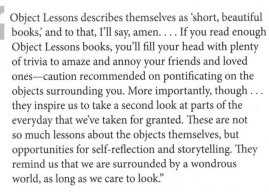

Object Lessons describes themselves as 'short, beautiful
books,' and to that, I'll say, amen. . . . If you read enough
Object Lessons books, you'll fill your head with plenty
of trivia to amaze and annoy your friends and loved
ones—caution recommended on pontificating on the
objects surrounding you. More importantly, though . . .
they inspire us to take a second look at parts of the
everyday that we've taken for granted. These are not
so much lessons about the objects themselves, but
opportunities for self-reflection and storytelling. They
remind us that we are surrounded by a wondrous
world, as long as we care to look."

John Warner, *The Chicago Tribune*

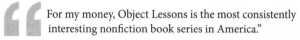

For my money, Object Lessons is the most consistently interesting nonfiction book series in America."

Megan Volpert, *PopMatters*

Besides being beautiful little hand-sized objects themselves, showcasing exceptional writing, the wonder of these books is that they exist at all . . . Uniformly excellent, engaging, thought-provoking, and informative."

Jennifer Bort Yacovissi, *Washington Independent Review of Books*

. . . edifying and entertaining . . . perfect for slipping in a pocket and pulling out when life is on hold."

Sarah Murdoch, *Toronto Star*

[W]itty, thought-provoking, and poetic . . . These little books are a page-flipper's dream."

John Timpane, *The Philadelphia Inquirer*

Though short, at roughly 25,000 words apiece, these books are anything but slight."

Marina Benjamin, *New Statesman*

> The joy of the series, of reading *Remote Control, Golf Ball, Driver's License, Drone, Silence, Glass, Refrigerator, Hotel,* and *Waste* . . . in quick succession, lies in encountering the various turns through which each of their authors has been put by his or her object. . . . The object predominates, sits squarely center stage, directs the action. The object decides the genre, the chronology, and the limits of the study. Accordingly, the author has to take her cue from the *thing* she chose or that chose her. The result is a wonderfully uneven series of books, each one a *thing* unto itself."

Julian Yates, *Los Angeles Review of Books*

> The Object Lessons series has a beautifully simple premise. Each book or essay centers on a specific object. This can be mundane or unexpected, humorous or politically timely. Whatever the subject, these descriptions reveal the rich worlds hidden under the surface of things."

Christine Ro, *Book Riot*

> . . . a sensibility somewhere between Roland Barthes and Wes Anderson."

Simon Reynolds, author of *Retromania: Pop Culture's Addiction to Its Own Past*

OBJECTLESSONS

A book series about the hidden lives of ordinary things.

Series Editors:

Ian Bogost and Christopher Schaberg

Advisory Board:

Sara Ahmed, Jane Bennett, Jeffrey Jerome Cohen, Johanna Drucker, Raiford Guins, Graham Harman, renée hoogland, Pam Houston, Eileen Joy, Douglas Kahn, Daniel Miller, Esther Milne, Timothy Morton, Kathleen Stewart, Nigel Thrift, Rob Walker, Michele White.

In association with

BOOKS IN THE SERIES

football

MARK YAKICH

BLOOMSBURY ACADEMIC
NEW YORK • LONDON • OXFORD • NEW DELHI • SYDNEY

BLOOMSBURY ACADEMIC
Bloomsbury Publishing Inc
1385 Broadway, New York, NY 10018, USA
50 Bedford Square, London, WC1B 3DP, UK
29 Earlsfort Terrace, Dublin 2, Ireland

BLOOMSBURY, BLOOMSBURY ACADEMIC and the Diana logo are trademarks
of Bloomsbury Publishing Plc

First published in the United States of America 2022

Cover design: Alice Marwick

For legal purposes the Acknowledgments on p. 163 constitute an extension
of this copyright page.

Bloomsbury Publishing Inc does not have any control over, or responsibility for, any
third-party websites referred to or in this book. All internet addresses given in this
book were correct at the time of going to press. The author and publisher regret
any inconvenience caused if addresses have changed or sites have ceased to exist,
but can accept no responsibility for any such changes.

A catalog record for this book is available from the Library of Congress.

Library of Congress Cataloging-in-Publication Data
Names: Yakich, Mark, author.
Title: Football / Mark Yakich.
Identifiers: LCCN 2021027331 (print) | LCCN 2021027332 (ebook) | ISBN
9781501367069 (Paperback) | ISBN 9781501367076 (ePub) | ISBN 9781501367083
(PDF) | ISBN 9781501367090 (eBook)
Subjects: LCSH: Football.
Classification: LCC GV951 .Y35 2022 (print) | LCC GV951 (ebook) |
DDC 796.33–dc23
LC record available at https://lccn.loc.gov/2021027331
LC ebook record available at https://lccn.loc.gov/2021027332

ISBN: PB: 978-1-5013-6706-9
ePDF: 978-1-5013-6708-3
eBook: 978-1-5013-6707-6

Series: Object Lessons

Typeset by Deanta Global Publishing Services, Chennai, India
Printed and bound in the United States of America

To find out more about our authors and books visit www.bloomsbury.com and sign
up for our newsletters.

for the Pandemic Players

CONTENTS

In football the worst blindness is only seeing the ball.
—NELSON FALCÃO RODRIGUES

1 INTRODUCTION TO A SLIGHTLY NEW GAME

It was the first week of April, and I hadn't planned on doing it. I'd gone for a run in Audubon Park in New Orleans, where I'd been running more and more since the stay-at-home order was mandated three weeks earlier. This time, I'd taken a route through the golf course closed to golfers but open to walkers, bikers, picnickers, solo karate practitioners, and anyone else who wanted to take up space on a fairway, bunker, or green. When I popped out the other side of the course, near the spot where I've played soccer on Sundays for a decade, I couldn't quite believe what I was seeing: four men, two 3' by 6' pop-up goals, and a ball.

It was beautiful and it was illegal. The mayor had just banned contact sports.

I stopped in my tracks.

"Where are your cleats?" asked Jimmy, one of the regulars.

"How's this gonna work?" I said.

"Just keep your six feet," he said. "It'll be okay."

"We did it last week," added Kanu, another regular. "You get only three touches, but you can shoot from anywhere."

"You playing, or what?" said John, a sometimes-regular who approached.

Another guy was standing nearby, on his phone. I didn't know him, but he was wearing cleats. I figured I'd better join before he took the fourth spot in the game of 2-a-side.

Between a live oak whose limbs barely touched the ground, as a kind of backstop, and a cedar sapling, we spaced the goals out about 40 yards. I tightened the laces on my running shoes. No one bothered to stretch, thinking, as I was, that surely someone in the hordes of walkers, or more likely park security would soon come over to squelch our little game.

The old bliss began the moment my foot made contact with the ball. Who needed shin pads or a mouthguard (I'd lost a tooth a few years back) or a sweatband? It had been three weeks without playing, without endorphins, endocannabinoids, dopamine, or whatever it was that my brain normally released from sprinting and kicking and trapping and falling for six or seven miles each Sunday from ten until noon or one, depending on how much familial scorn I felt I could tolerate once I returned home.

After a couple of series up and down our mini-pitch, I said, "The three-touch rule is changing my entire game—I can't attack on defense like I usually do."

John said, "This is going to show who knows how to use space."

"It's all about cutting off angles," said Kanu.

Jimmy said nothing. He was busy finding the space and angle to put the ball into the back of the net from a distance.

We played for an hour and a half, the score something like 10-7. I put in the final goal, a left-footed chip from twenty yards out, a small miracle.

Usually after the game ended, we would high-five and embrace each other. This time we didn't even elbow-bump. We said awkward goodbyes. On my walk home, I tried to replay the match in my head, the accurate passes, the feints, the stunning shots; but my mind kept coming back to one thing: the moment I'd accidentally violated the six-feet rule in defending John. I could still feel his wet shoulder brushing against my arm. Could one get the virus from sweat? From body odor? If I could smell my buddy's deodorant, wouldn't that mean that possible virus molecules were passing through my sinuses and into my lungs?

Then a graver thought: Should I tell my wife I played?

At home, I admitted that I "kicked the ball around with a couple of guys in the park." She nodded. I didn't expand.

The same day the following week I returned to the spot in the park, but only a few sunbathers were there. I was so disappointed that I didn't finish my run, just turned around and moped home.

The following week I couldn't get myself to go for a run.

But a week later, it was Sunday morning again. I'd been in a bad slump for five days in a row. Genuine depression, the kind I knew well from four years earlier, after both my parents died—the kind where one can't get out of bed and if one does, because one has to help with three small children, one finds oneself laying down before noon on any available flat surface hidden from the gaze of others. I knew I couldn't afford a sixth day, the turning point into full-blown numbness, in which profound sadness would be a welcome relief.

I put on my turf shoes, and began to fumblingly confess to my wife what I was going to do.

"It's all right," she said. I looked up.

"Go," she said.

I didn't run. I rode my bike, with my ball bouncing around in the milk crate jerry-rigged to the back rack.

In the park, from a distance, I thought I could make out the small nets and players. My heart may or may not have raced. When I got close enough, the bike just fell out from beneath me, crashing to the ground, and I yelled: "Can I play!"

John yelled back: "Did you bring a kid?"

I tried to fathom his words, then glanced over to the spot: a few kids and our friend Jimmy lingered.

"You have to bring one of your kids to play. The virus and all. We have to limit the bubble."

I didn't really understand the logic of bringing more people—bubble or no bubble. But I did wish that my twelve-year-old son, a very good soccer player, would come out and play too. I was having trouble even getting him to kick the ball back and forth with me on the sidewalk in front of our house.

Jimmy walked over.

"Fuck it," he smiled, "we'll make an exception."

From that day on, a handful of the old regulars began playing as much as possible—once, twice, then three times each week. Soon I found myself bringing the ball, pop-up nets, and pinnies, and coordinating group messaging so that everyone knew when and where we'd play. It still wasn't technically legal, but we took the risk. I had a new personal risk as well: the tendonitis in my right knee, for which I'd been doing physical therapy for five months, was becoming a chronic condition. After two weeks the tendon below my left kneecap also became inflamed. It couldn't be helped. This was the pandemic. Nothing, it seemed, could be helped. But the thing about chronic conditions is that some of them turn positive; even if I could no longer watch professionals play live games, I could live in this new moment if I kept playing the game—chronically.

2 A CONCESSION

It strikes me a bit funny that a number of well-known books about the sport begin the same way—with a concession. "I was the worst wooden leg ever to set foot on the little soccer fields of my country," says Eduardo Galeano on the first page of *Football in Sun and Shadow*. "I suck at soccer," writes Franklin Foer in the first sentence of *How Soccer Explains the World*.

I don't suck. I began playing at age eight when my mother drove me to a neighboring Chicago suburb to try a sport she'd never heard of, and ten years later I started at left fullback for my college team. But I was never good enough to play professionally, and never did I want to. I'm not a rabid fan, or even a fan of a particular club. And there's a whole swath of history about football of which I have only cursory knowledge. To be frank, there were years when I didn't think about the game very much—while I was in my late twenties and early thirties living overseas, or in graduate school, obsessed instead with reading and writing poems. But football came back for me. In fact, I suspect it was underneath the surface of my being the whole time. Which sounds rather hokey. But the pandemic has turned even hokeyness on its ear. Outside of my family, football is now the most reliable and consistent presence in my life—and its facets keep opening up to me.

For example, one evening, weeks into lockdown, as I was lamenting the absence of live football broadcasts, I came across "blind football." I began watching YouTube videos of pre-pandemic matches, utterly entranced. The game is played on futsal pitches (essentially the same size as a basketball court), with four outfield players, each wearing eye shades to maintain fairness in case a player can detect some light, and one goalkeeper who may be partially blind but more often is sighted. As with the indoor soccer I played as a teenager, there are boards on the perimeter of the pitch facilitating a continual play. The ball's panels are equipped with metal bearings so that the ball can be heard and located; the sound is a cross between a tambourine and the jingling of coins in a pants pocket. Perhaps most important, all fans remain silent during play.

I remained mesmerized by player after player, who seemed to roller skate across the turf, their insteps handling the ball as though they were playing ping-pong. As I imagined how a defender must defend by sound and what must be vacillations of air currents, I began to comprehend the virtually unlimited nature and adaptation of the game of football. Long past midnight I watched, drifting into an equanimity equal to any I've known during years of practicing yoga and meditation.

3 THE NAME OF THE GAME

What I love about The Beautiful Game is that I didn't know it was called "The Beautiful Game" until I'd played it for more than thirty years. I love, too, that outside of authors of books about football, nobody who plays or watches the sport refers to it by that moniker—just as nobody who lives in New Orleans calls it "The Big Easy."

The Sunday morning match I've played for years is technically a pickup game, "pickup" connoting a take-it or leave-it quality. While the game is open to anyone—men, women, even at times a pre-teen or two—the game is anything but random, anything but inconsequential. The match is far better than any religious service, and when I miss it, the whole week seems to be off-kilter, like I'm being punished for not running around the pitch madly for hours.

Over the years I have suffered innumerable, inglorious bangs and cuts and knocks, a pair of bruised ribs, a concussion, a torn PCL, and a broken tooth. Three weeks ago, a hornet bit me in the right butt cheek as I was retrieving the ball from a thick patch of hosta plants. The welt lasted a week and there's still a scar where the stinger went in.

What I love about the game is that I no longer tell my wife how it went—and certainly not about the injuries. After the damaged knee and subsequent months of physical therapy, she urged me to quit playing. I found myself stumbling to explain the game's importance to my well-being. I may have used the word "survival." I know that she was well-intentioned in her admonishing, worrying about my body as I approached age fifty; but she couldn't quite grasp what I said about my mental health, even as a licensed therapist.

Except for when I was an expat in Europe and variously called the game *le foot* (France) or *Fußball* (Germany) or football (UK), I know the game as soccer. That name derives from "soc," a slang term for "association" as in association football, the name the game was given to distinguish it from "rugby football." Besides in the US, other countries also often call it soccer or a variation of soccer in translation, including Australia, South Africa, Japan, Korea, and much of Southeast Asia. In 2014, a Redditor named reddripper devised a world map to parse out the name of the game.[1]

---

[1]The Reddit thread generated hundreds of comments: discrepancies and proprietary arguments over what the game is called in various locales. https://www.reddit.com/r/soccer/comments/1tg14k/football_vs_soccer_how_people_of_the_world_name/

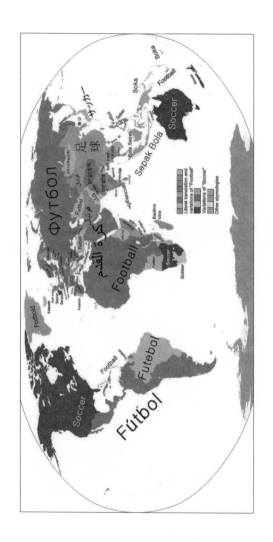

Notice the patches where people call it neither soccer nor football. For example, in Italy it's called *calcio* ("to kick") and in Indonesia it's called *sepak bola* ("kick ball"). Excepting baseball in the States, what happens colloquially is that people often call the game simply "ball," as in "let's go play ball" or "the kids are outside playing ball." Ball here refers to one thing: the world's most popular sport. In other words, the confusion about the game's name isn't really confusion; it's evidence of the sport's popularity. Played by 250 million and watched by 1 billion, The Beautiful Game is comparable to no other sport for its global as well as local reach.[2]

---

[2] The stats on "popularity" for sports are fluid. Some put the estimated fans at 3.5 billion for soccer since "popularity" might encompass watching and playing. In any and all cases, association football comes out on top, and cricket second. And if you, as a US citizen, are wondering: baseball ranks seventh; basketball and American football around ninth, each with between 400 and 500 million fans. https://www.topendsports.com/world/lists/popular-sport/fans.htm

4 POPULARITY, CONTESTS

Despite its popularity some people hate it—or are at least dubious about the endeavor. "What kind of game is this [anyway] for old ladies and fairies? I quit," intones Sylvester Stallone's character in the 1981 movie *Victory*. The poor Yank POW has to tackle (as in American football-tackle) an opposing player just to get the attention of the British POW captain/coach Michael Caine. Caine wants to beat the Nazis in a football match; Stallone wants to use the match as a means of escaping the Nazis.

Even some people who love the game have had to hide their true feelings about it. "I'd played soccer all my life," writes the novelist and painter Rabih Alameddine. "I used to joke when I first moved to San Francisco that I had an easier time coming out as gay to my straight friends than telling my gay friends that I loved soccer."[1]

---

[1]Rabih Alameddine, "How to Bartend," *Lit Hub*, April 8, 2020. https://lithub.com/how-to-bartend/

In the 1980s in my US high school, both soccer players and gays (the word "queer" had not yet been reclaimed) were suspect. Clean-cut American football players looked down on us scrawny soccer players. I never understood it: they were clad in thick pads and helmets while our only armor were baggy Umbro shorts and unkempt mullets. Which one of us appeared weaker? Now that concussions in American football are out in the open, I suppose the whole point is moot. Or the point is that premature death is a good enough reason to play soccer instead of American football.[2]

Why association football took so long to take off in the US, and that it still lags behind most other parts of the world still seems to be a perennial subject of arguments and dissertations. It can be fun to speculate like Andrei Markovits and Lars Rensmann do in the last chapter of *Gaming the World*:

> Put crudely but, we believe, correctly, had Harvard joined Yale and the other private East Coast colleges in forming a football league in 1873 (that would have continued to feature the Association game which all these colleges already play), college soccer, not college football, would

---

[2]Today we often think of American football as all-domineering in the States, but as Ian Plenderleith reminds us in the introduction to *Rock 'n' Roll Soccer: The Short Life and Fast Times of North American Soccer League*, in the first decades after WWII, the most popular sports in the US were baseball, boxing, and horseracing (p. 3).

have become the passion of many millions of American sports fans over the past 150 years and the country would have developed into the one of the premier soccer powers of the world.[3]

Markovits and Rensmann go on for six more pages about how the Harvard boys (and their faculty) initially had played the Boston Common game (i.e., association football) until a fateful trip to Montreal to play McGill in their kind of "football" (i.e., rugby) led Harvard to abandon soccer altogether for rugby.

There are many lines of thought about soccer's "growth problem" in the States, ranging from cultural reasons (people in the States can't stand a game "without a clear winner") to historical ones (the US jettisoned Britain's colonial rule before the advent of the game) to systemic ones (a lack of coordinated youth academies in the States). I'm not convinced the issue is such a mystery. The problem isn't that the sport lacks popularity; it's that there are so many other sports in the world to compete with. As well, the world has grown exponentially more complex, and complex things are messy and often feel unknowable. One of my colleagues continually used to ask me why poetry isn't as popular as it once was— "during Robert Frost's time or Sylvia Plath's time." I think

---

[3]Markovits and Rensmann, *Gaming the World: How Sports Are Reshaping Global Politics and Culture* (Princeton UP, 2013), 296.

he'd missed what was right in front of him: that the world has become increasingly varied and interconnected! It's not that poetry is no longer popular—it's that so many other things are popular now too, including contemporary music, movies and TV series, video games, and all those other activities and entertainments that vie for our attention. The aggregate number of poetry readers in the US is much greater than it was in, say, 1930 or 1960 or 1990, and so too is the aggregate number of US soccer fans and players.

One might come at this entire debate from another angle: it's perfectly okay that soccer isn't the most popular sport here. For better or worse, we don't always need America to be first. In fact, when people say "America" they mean the United States, as though the other countries and peoples of the Americas don't exist. This isn't semantics. Or rather it is: the words we use on a daily basis to name and to describe and to think embody how we view ourselves and others, and how—whether we are aware of it or not—we promote certain ways of thinking over others. If in the US the Super Bowl crowns a "world champion," it's a funny kind of champion, since virtually nobody plays "American" football outside of the United States. If baseball ends its season with "The World Series," it's equally a limited world.

In men's football in Europe, the most prestigious tournament is the Champions League. Begun in 1955 as the European Cup, the tournament features top-tier club teams from across Europe that battle it out each year for a single winner. The 2020 champion was Bayern Munich who bested

Paris Saint Germain 1-0 in Lisbon in a fanless stadium. Real Madrid has won the tournament the most times (13); Christiano Ronaldo has collected the trophy five times (once with Manchester United and four times with Real Madrid), and Lionel Messi has done so with Barcelona four times. Winning your country's club league title (whether first division, second, etc.) is what all clubs aim for each season, but winning the Champions League is what few clubs can even dream about. Underlying all the talk of champions (world or otherwise) is something football language guru Frank Seddon reminds us of:

> From the thirteenth century, a knight or other nominee sent on to a duelling field to fight a "trial by battle" on his master's behalf came to be called a *champion*, derived from *campus*, Latin for "field." It also gave us the recreational activity *camping*, which . . . was once the East Anglian name for "football." Also *campaign*, via the French *campagne*, for countryside, literally "a march through the land" . . . All of which field-related trivia should serve to remind you, next time you're moved to chant "Champions!," what it's all about. Homage to "mercenaries who earn their living fighting battles on fields on behalf of others, their ultimate paymasters"—that's professional football.[4]

---

[4]*Football Talk: The Language & Folklore of the World's Greatest Game* (London: Robson Books, 2004), 27.

5 STANDSTILL

Right now nobody is playing any professional sports. By "right now" I mean during the COVID-19 pandemic, or the time of the coronavirus, or the plague, or whatever one feels like naming it on this day, April 30, 2020, a month after I signed the contract for the book you are reading. Today— like yesterday and the days before that in which the day-of-the-week meant less and less—is anything but ordinary. Healthcare workers are doing their jobs, garbage collectors are doing theirs, and politicians and civil servants are doing good or bad jobs, depending on one's mood. One thing is objectively accurate: professional footballers aren't playing professional games. They aren't taking planes or trains or buses. Maybe some of them are riding stationary bicycles to stay in shape (maintaining large thighs is important). Maybe not. Today is exactly like that: at once a very large and very tiny *may-be*.

I'm actually glad that the game is at a standstill because I can read all the books about football that I've never read, and I don't have to worry about following the plethora of current matches—in Europe, the States, Latin America, or Asia. The fact is, until last year, I'd never cracked open a book about football. I just played it, which didn't seem like a problem until I decided to write a book about it. Only then did I realize my ignorance as I walked the stacks of two university libraries, taking down dozens and dozens of books that academics, commentators, players, managers, and fans had penned about nearly every possible aspect of the sport—from cultural histories to tactical ones, from first-person narratives of playing and watching and coaching and refereeing to deep-dives into the politics (and even militarization) of the game, its fandom (rabid, measured, passive), its local and global economic ramifications, its endless and renewable dramas . . . and of course its history.

In reading countless books about football, I discovered much more variability that I expected. I suppose I didn't really know what to expect; the history of the sport is often told in a linear fashion even if what actually happened isn't quite so—a function of retelling. I soon became interested and then mystified as to why some fans become disgruntled whenever a new variation or rule is introduced or experimented with. Those who remonstrate *Don't tamper with the game!* have forgotten or perhaps never knew that the game has continually been tampered with—and not just recently in terms of masks, virus testing, increased substitutions, and fanless stadiums. In the early days of the modern game, you could only pass the ball laterally and backwards—no forward passes allowed. In fact, dribbling was the main action of the game until 1872 when a Scottish team felt they couldn't compete with their English opponent and began *passing*.[1] When I think of today's game, there seems to be no greater change than the back-pass rule set down in 1992. This was the same year the Premier League launched as well as the year I graduated college . . . meaning as a fullback on my college team whenever I got into trouble, I'd kick the ball back to my keeper who'd simply scoop it up into his arms without penalty. The future may hold an even greater change: with each new study on concussions, researchers, ex-players, and parents increasingly advocate for a change regarding heading the ball. There may come a time when players wear some kind of headband to mitigate head injuries, or even a time when heading the ball is no longer part of the game.

Before the laws of the modern game were laid down in England, there were what one might call "precursors," ranging from the Chinese ball game called *cuju* to the Japanese counterpart *kemari* to the omnipresence of various ball games, such as *pok-a-tok*, that were played in ball courts throughout Mesoamerica before Europeans arrived.[2] You can

---

[1] Laurent Dubois has a fine narrative of passing's early development in *The Language of the Game: How to Understand Soccer* (New York: Basic Books, 2018), 65-68.

[2] Some of these games used balls made with bladders; in certain Inuit groups the outer shell was made of sealskin and the inside stuffed with moss or deer hair. Only in Mesoamerica were balls made of solid rubber. Today, about 70% of the world's footballs are made in one city: Sialkot, Pakistan,

research the ancestry of football and come up with all kinds of curiosities. When I learned, for instance, that one of the sport's antecedents was called "mob football," a contemporary term for a medieval game in Europe where player and observer were interchangeable, where it was essentially less a game and more a phenomenon involving a ball batted about chaotically and played between villages, which had almost no parameters except against manslaughter or murder, I began to think about all the ways a virus could have easily passed from person to person back then, very unlike a ball.

The ball at that time, by the way, was often a pig's bladder. Or it was a pig's bladder—the inflated element of the ball—covered in animal hide. The oldest extant ball, about half the size of today's, was discovered in 1981 behind paneling in the Queen's bedchamber in Stirling Castle, Scotland. The ball dates from about 1540, and no one knows why exactly it was hidden.[3]

This historical trivia seemed trivial to me until I mentioned it to Rodolfo, a dear friend and fellow footballer. He explained how it sounds like the ball he and his friends

---

where more than 1,000 factories produce them, and where there is a not uncomplicated history of making footballs stretching back more than one hundred years. See "Where Soccer Gets Made," by Omar Waraich: https://ro adsandkingdoms.com/2018/where-soccer-gets-made/

[3]"The World's Oldest Football," accessed April, 14, 2020, http://www.bbc.co .uk/ahistoryoftheworld/objects/dYJ9eIf5QVagcSv4vUAh0Q

made as kids in Mozambique in the 1990s. "But," he added, "we used a condom."

"Condom?"

"For the bladder. Should we make one together for Gabe and Jonah?"

He was speaking about our four-year-old sons. I said I hadn't bought a condom in ages, having been married for almost 20 years, and asked him, not entirely joking, how large the condom should be. We laughed harder than we should have for one reason: we were living in a time when both everything and nothing seemed imaginable. And there was little hiding from our imaginations.

6 HOW TO MAKE A FOOTBALL

My 50th birthday occurred during the crescendo of Zoom: May 2020. I drank in fits and starts throughout morning and midday, which segued into a small gathering of friends on the sidewalk outside our home and later about twenty video rectangles of old friends on a screen. Seeing faces and hearing voices felt like good enough gifts. But it was Rodolfo who provided the most tangible one—in the form of a balloon, a plastic bag, a skein of yarn, and the promise of a lesson in making a football. Growing up in Mozambique, Rodolfo had made hundreds of footballs which he and his friends would play with. But he'd not made one for more than 15 years—we'd talked about making one together for months and simply didn't have the opportunity—until the coronavirus lockdown.

A week after my birthday, there we were both hunched over computers, Zooming with our respective small sons in our laps. My son, Jonah, held the three components.

"Condoms are better," Rodolfo said, picking up his balloon. "They're made not to break of course—you can get 10 liters of water in a condom."

He blew up the balloon, and I followed suit.

His seemed huge on the screen, and I suspected it was distorted, like how the actual size of a fish is exaggerated by holding it closer to the camera. When his son held the balloon, it looked a lot smaller.

I held up my own green balloon to Jonah's bowl-cut: "Is the size of a boy's head about right?"

He laughed, "That'll do."

We tied off our balloons, put them inside the plastic bags and tucked in the parts of the bag that stuck out, trying to get the surface as smooth around as possible. After wrestling the skein of yarn from Jonah, I began to wind it around the balloon/bag contraption.

"It'll look squat at first, like a pumpkin," Rodolfo said, "but just wrap the yarn the other direction."

I had my doubts that my pumpkin was going to turn into a sphere at some point. I imitated how Rodolfo pulled yarn around the other axis. The transformation was beginning to happen, except there were plastic bag bits poking out in places. I mentioned how another friend grew up in the Soviet Union and they'd made soccer balls out of balloons pasted over with papier-mâché. We speculated that that might not work so well in the rain.

"It's funny," he said, winding his ball, "I remember something—hold it to your chest as you wrap the yarn. It'll keep the ball tight."

Things improved.

"How long will it last?" I said.

"Ten to fourteen days," he said.

I held up my ball for him to see.

"Looking good!"

I admitted that a couple of strands had come loose. He said to wind more yarn over them, back into the ball. Then he added: "If we didn't have yarn, sometimes we'd find an old sweater and pull it apart."

Jonah began to worry that the ball/balloon might pop— like the flimsy water balloons he'd been making lately—so he decided to cast a magic spell on our balls.

Rodolfo and I listened intently for the first ten seconds of abracadabras which soon devolved into a babble of naming whatever was in sight in the room—children's books, a rainbow painting over the bed, a stuffed animal frog, the neighbor's pine tree visible out the window, his mother's bra draped over a doorknob, etc. It was a strange soliloquy, but Rodolfo and I were used to waiting things out. This was the eighth or ninth (?) week of lockdown. Patience was no longer a virtue; it was merely one facet of endurance.

Then, Rodolfo got called away—his wife was on another video call with her dad. I knew his mother-in-law was on a ventilator up in Boston. But it wasn't COVID-19. She had recently been experiencing neck pain and paralysis, and finally received a diagnosis of Guillain-Barré Syndrome. There was also their other son, a one-year-old, to deal with. I assured Rodolfo that I'd keep working on the wrap-job until he could call back.

"There's a special zig-zag technique to do at the end." He said it with special delight, as though it was the key to unlocking the universe.

Jonah wanted to know why they had to hang up. When I took too long to answer, he said, "Did Mr. Rodolfo get the virus? I know all about the virus. And hawks. Hawks and the virus."

I wasn't sure how hawks got involved, but I assured him that our friends were okay.

While he went off to the kitchen yelling "NEED SNACK!", I continued emptying the skein of yarn around and around the ball.

The repetitive motion of winding was beginning to shoot pain into my left arm, near the elbow. I'd been getting physical therapy before quarantine, and periodically when I did something "wrong" it would flare up. I tried to ignore it.

I tried to enjoy the boredom of what I was doing. Round and round, trying to get the thing to look less oblong, more spherical. The task focused my mind, and soon I was thinking about Rodolfo and how he was feeling about making his ball, instructing me on mine. I thought of the stories he'd told me over the year and a half of our friendship: how little he and his nine siblings had growing up, his father's physical abuse toward his mother and himself, the things he never recounted to me with even the slightest amount of self-pity. I thought about how he always thanks me for asking him how his family is doing, how work is going, or how his health is. For years in his late teens and twenties, he had very low energy, trouble thinking clearly, and memory problems. When he came to the States five years ago, he saw a doctor for the first time in a decade. In a matter of days, it was determined he was vitamin B12 deficient. He received vitamin B12 injections and suddenly was a new person—his old self.

A few minutes later, Rodolfo called back. "Leave about 10 feet of yarn."

I unwrapped some, and he walked me through how to take the yarn under and over a particularly tight patch of yarn on one side of the ball, repeating the same on the other side, and zig-zagging such anchor points all around the ball until the final tie-off.

I tossed it up and down gently. The air-filled balloon inside was the bladder, the plastic bag was the inner membrane, and the yarn made up the outer shell—the latter seemed key to giving the ball the right weight distribution. And when I stood and dropped it to my feet and kicked it over to Jonah, the touch of the ball felt perfect.

Jonah brought the ball back up to the computer.

Rodolfo exclaimed, "That looks good. You're a natural!"

I told him how the texture of the ball was like felt, similar to the balls I'd played indoor soccer with as a teenager.

"It might deflate a little in a day or two," he said.

I didn't care. I was inordinately happy.

Before he had to end our call again and return to life at home, I thanked Rodolfo for his gift. He did what he usually does: he thanked me for thanking him.

With our new ball, Jonah headed down the hallway to the front room where we'd repurposed two small hockey nets for soccer, the hockey sticks long ago closeted and taken out only to retrieve matchbox cars that get stuck under the fridge.

Matchbox cars. Jonah must have at least a hundred of them—my old steel ones made in England, new plastic ones from China, others of unknown make from garage sales and Salvation Army stores. Then the thought: Rodolfo had a single Matchbox car as a kid. He kept it hidden in a special spot, taking it out when no one else was around. It was the one thing, he'd once told me, that was all his.

I watched Jonah kick the ball into the net over and over. I decided not to interrupt. It was lockdown after all, and rare to have him entertained without my having to entertain him.

Later, when he abandoned it to go hunt for lizards outside, I picked up the ball to get a closer look. It was homemade. It was novel. It was almost too pretty to play with.

I held it up toward the wall, and snapped a photo. The ball might not last very long, but the photo would—and from a distance, it almost looked like the World Cup trophy.[1]

---

[1] Author photo, May 2020.

7 TWO GAMES

I've watched American football on TV since I was a little kid—far more than I have watched soccer. My first, and still primary, hero is the legendary running back of the 1970s and 80s Chicago Bears: Walter Payton. Over the decades his two interchangeable mottos have stuck with me: "Never give up" and "Never die easy." When my eldest son was a toddler and would fall down or fail at some task, I'd show him YouTube videos of Walter Payton escaping tackles and innumerable defenders. I told him to be like Walter Payton, and that I'd already installed a "Walter Payton button" inside him so that whenever he needed extra energy all he had to do was press that button—which came with an accompanying *diddle-liddle-liddle* sound.

The point is, I've incorporated more American football-type metaphors and patterns into my mental life than those of other sports. I know all the game's rules and can throw an excellent spiral and even played a weekly game of two-hand-touch in Audubon Park for a couple of years. And yet, I don't understand the finer aspects of the game: I never played on an organized team in school, or memorized a playbook, or donned pads and a helmet. Although it may seem obvious that watching the game of American football is very different than playing the game "recreationally," TV broadcasters rarely talk about it.

The same goes for association football. One watches the sport and thinks one is seeing and experiencing the game, but it's all on the outside. In other words, there are two different kinds of football. There's the professional game that we watch from the couch on a TV or in bed on a screen or from the seats in a billion-dollar stadium. And then there's the informal game in a park or street watched by an occasional passerby. One is dependent on finances, economies of scale, academies or college teams, and vast numbers of people who are not players—managers and coaching staffs, as well as executives, marketers, publicists, sports journalists, accountants, medical professionals, stadium workers, etc. The other is independent of those things. One is glamorous, dramatic, and written about daily. The other is anything but.

The regular pickup game in which I play doesn't include corner kicks, throw-ins, or goalkeepers. Slide-tackles aren't permitted, though the game still had plenty of shoulder-to-shoulder play and physicality. There are no referees; we make our own calls. Although we keep score, I usually don't know it. And the men and women I play with rarely talk about the Premier League, La Liga, Bundesliga, Brazil's Big Twelve, Liga MX, Japan's J.League, NWSL, or any of the other professional leagues around the world. The closest MLS club is a five-hour drive away in Houston, and the local club, the

New Orleans Jesters, is a fourth division squad. I've taken my son to only one of their matches; he was invited to be one of the ball boys, which I probably found more fun than he did.

How do fans fit into these two games? In pickup games there are no fans, unless one considers players cheering each other on "fans." As for professional football, the eminent and articulate *New York Times* soccer correspondent Rory Smith writes:

> As anyone who has ever watched a game in an empty stadium will know, it is when the shouts of the coaches echo clearly around a ground, when goals are scored and only a handful of people halfheartedly celebrate them, that it becomes clear that it is fans who give soccer not just its background, but its meaning.

My simple reply is *maybe*. Smith published the piece featuring that paragraph on March 6, 2020, just as countries were going into lockdown. If anything has become clearer since then, it's that individuals and the societies they compose can become acclimated to almost anything, including playing professional sports without fans.

Live football matches, in fact, were the first "public" events to return after the first lockdowns. In early May 2020, South Korea's K-League kicked off matches inside stadiums without supporters . . . though in their haste officials filled some of the seats with inflatable dolls which turned out to be sex dolls. In Germany and other countries, clubs experimented with cardboard cut-out fans propped up in stadium seats. In a month or two, everyone got used to colorful banners draped over seats and green screen technology in place of live fans, and broadcasters ceased saying things like, "It's all so weird!" or, "This is odd, isn't it?" If it wasn't business as usual, it was still business. In other words, football was and is a system with rules and conventions that can and will change. The biggest problem is the business part: how to keep the money flowing which requires large quantities of fans and, pre-virus, very fancy stadiums.

Football stadiums are bigger and better than ever, if one defines better as more expensive. In 2007, London's Wembley Stadium cost $1.5 billion to build. In 2014, Singapore National Stadium came in at $1.3 billion. These numbers aren't exclusive to association football. Most recently, the Allegiant Stadium in Paradise, Nevada, cost $2 billion to construct. As I sat down to watch the inaugural game between the Saints and the Raiders on Monday Night Football, I noted the sideline broadcaster's glee in touting the stadium's "luxury." Part of the luxury is a retractable natural grass field that resides in a four-foot-deep "tray." The tray remains outside the edifice most of the time to catch sunlight, and then is slid into the domed stadium for games. Super cool and high-tech, I thought, until the broadcaster mentioned the stadium's nickname: the Death Star. This was September 21, 2020: none of the 65,000 gleaming stadium seats were filled with fans, and COVID-19 related deaths had reached 200,000 in the US that morning.

Even though I regularly play the game of football, sports marketers would call me a "casual fan." I delight in the thrill of attending a professional sports event to enjoy the hyper-expensive tricked-out stadiums, and to take part in an event vastly larger than myself; but I seldom do it. The consultancy group Deloitte offers this about "fan engagement":

> In today's world, building it is not enough to make them come. In order to win fans today and to keep them coming back into the future, stadiums not only need to get the basics right . . . they should elevate the experience as stadiums compete with the home experience . . . powered by better camera angles, the growth of augmented reality/virtual reality (AR/VR), and multi-platform, multimedia experiences. At the same time, the monetary cost and time commitment of stadium attendance remains high. As a result, while revenues for teams have steadily increased, stadium attendance has stagnated or decreased slightly across many of the leagues studied.[1]

In October 2020, I woke up one morning at three o'clock in order to tune into a webinar about changes in broadcasting,

---

[1] "The stadium experience: Keeping sports fans engaged—and loyal," accessed on March 4, 2021, https://www2.deloitte.com/us/en/pages/technol ogy-media-and-telecommunications/articles/stadium-experience-fan-satis faction-survey.html

streaming, and value-added content, titled "The Importance of AI in the Sports Industry."[2] From India, Spain, and France, company owners and project managers promoted their ventures in monetizing at-home fans. The first speaker declared, "Gen Z doesn't i.d. with being a fan, instead they like video games. If the NBA doesn't look like Fortnight, then more fans will look at Fortnight than the NBA." The next proposed, "What's the market value of a football player in real-time? If we can offer that on-screen as a game is happening, it would be like following the stock market but in humans. If a player makes a mistake, misses a pass, you can make a live-bet and see that player's worth."

He was talking about doubling-down on live-betting: gambling sites that allow you to bet as a match is happening on, say, which team will score first, which player will score next, at what time the next goal will occur, what the score will be at halftime based on the current score, and so on. New analytics and high-speed tech, this gentleman contended, could allow for micro live-bets as well as synching bets to a player's "value." The discussion of monetization went on from there, supported by sophisticated charts and graphs.

I was becoming increasingly horrified. I understood the value of data-crunching to improve predictability so that teams can "play better" together or "get an advantage" over other teams, and especially to prevent individual players

---

[2]The Importance of AI in the Sports Industry. October 22, 2020. Webinar.

from getting injuries. From data collected about on-pitch performance to what players are eating and doing in their non-football time, every piece of information that's possible to attain about a player is being analyzed and algorithmized for even the slightest edge. Why? Because the tiniest margin often separates the winners from losers. And winning is important because it translates into money. The more you win, the more fans and sponsors are pleased, the more fans and sponsors you gain—the more the more the more.

But a question kept nagging at me: What is it that we want from football? Love? Money? Everything?

The next week the issue opened up before me as I was watching Barcelona lose to Getafe CF. Ray Hudson, an analyst I usually appreciate, began going on and on about one of Barcelona's strikers: "He's a 140 million Euro player, and he's not playing up to the price tag!" I thought: Who can play up to that number? And even if someone can play up to it, what are we saying about that person? Then I recalled what happened right before La Liga began its new season. At the end of August, Lionel Messi, the player all variations of Barcelona have been built around for the past 15 years, announced his deep desire to leave the club. However, not long afterward it became obvious: he couldn't go anywhere. Nobody could or wanted to pay the 700 million Euro fee to the club in order to acquire him. In other words, Messi stayed not for love of Barça and not even for money—because it wasn't money he was seeking. He wanted new management, new teammates, and a new coach that would enable him to "compete" at the highest level. He stayed because there wasn't much of a choice. The financial system was so profit-oriented that even Barcelona's owners were unable to make decisions: a locked-in system of contracts and potential legal disputes meant nothing would change. This would seem to be a variation on "systemic bias"; a certain kind of data (finances, profit margins) becomes a tyranny but with no specific tyrant to point to. In other words, the monetization of players can be so efficient that it outpaces a club's economic means.

I cannot pretend to have any expertise about the financial pyramid of professional football, and I have no answers about what fans are supposed to make of it all. I admit to being the casual fan. I admit also that when I do read news articles or hear broadcasters talk about money and football, I retreat to the other game: pickup. Perhaps fan engagement consultants have it somewhat backwards. Instead of trying to figure out how to enhance the live experience in stadiums or monetizing at-home viewers, they might focus on how to turn more fans into at-home players—pickup players. Not a perfect parallel, but I have seen this happen in poetry: an excellent way to get more people to read poems is to encourage them to write their own. It improves the private experience of reading, as well as the public world of poetry.

8 90-MINUTE MEDS

My father starved to death due to rectal cancer, and my mother died less than a year later due to multiple organ failure. This is merely true, and in no way unique to me. The fact that my grief work extended past the six months allotted by my gastroenterologist-psychiatrist, and that my wife and I were expecting our third child was also nothing special. The out-of-body panic attack I experienced, however, in the middle of teaching John Keats' "This Living Hand" sent me across a psychic line I've never quite been able to get back over.

That evening, when I managed to get home after class, I lay myself gently down on the sofa as though any slight move might shatter my insides. When I was able to tell my wife what happened—that I thought I was going to die right there in front of my students and that I still had the feeling—she nodded and took care of the children. When they all went to bed, I turned on the TV. There was a football match. It didn't matter who was playing whom, and I didn't really watch as much as I followed the spherical object around the pitch as it pinballed off players, trying to remain absolutely still as any movement made things worse. The match ended. I began another. At some point, I got on my hands and knees and crawled to the bedroom and into bed.

The next morning the uncanny feeling had subsided by half, but over the next week it would rise again in waves. Each time, when I was at home, I would go back to the TV and find a match and follow the ball and re-anchor myself. This pattern continued over weeks and into months. Usually one match was enough, though sometimes an accompanying Xanax would have to be procured from a stash a friend had given me. When the Xanax ran out, I still had the TV and the matches.

To this day, the most important aspect of watching remains the fact that everything is in play, a present ongoingness of ninety minutes. Except for a 15-minute halftime break, there are no timeouts and very few moments of non-play. If a player is injured and goes down, medical staff run out and get him or her off the pitch as soon as possible and play goes on. If there's a video review, broadcasters moan when it's not dispensed within a matter of seconds. If managers want to give players advice, they have to yell it from their technical area on the sideline. (Though, Borussia Dortmund's ex-manager Lucien Favre used to send in handwritten notes with substitutes who then passed the messages on. I always wondered what the players did with the scraps of paper after reading them, until one match when a camera zoomed in for a languorous moment on the still life of a tiny wad of paper nestled in green grass.)

Because the clock never stops, watching the game on a broadcast allows for the most wondrous thing: the absence of commercials. Other sports, such as basketball or ice hockey, may have a "flowing" game or "beautiful" plays, but only football allows the game to genuinely ebb and free-flow for extended periods of time without capitalist intervention. In American football, by comparison, the NFL requires 20 "television timeouts" per game, each lasting a minute or two.

Soccer is not entirely advert-free. When you watch a match on a screen, you observe capitalism on the fringes: perimeter boards or pitch-side LED-banners. It can be startling to see, for instance, adverts for the oil and gas mega-corporation Gazprom or the online gambling giant bet365 or the home improvement company Screwfix buzzing and flashing behind a striker sprinting down the sideline in counterattack. More noticeable, across the chests of players there are no mascots or icons, such as falcons or fleur-de-lis. Instead, companies and corporate entities are prominently displayed: recently, for example, Rakuten on Barcelona's jerseys, Etihad Airways on Mumbai City's, and Herbalife Nutrition on LA Galaxy's. Clubs in Liga MX, Mexico's top league and the fourth most popular in the world, are particularly tattooed with brands. For the 2019-20 season, Club León had 11 logos placed on its kits from collar, chest, back, and sleeve, to socks and shorts.[1]

---

[1]"Insane—Here Is Which Liga MX Team Kits Have The Most Kit Sponsors," August 10, 2019. https://www.footyheadlines.com/2019/08/insane-here-is -which-liga-mx-team-kits-have-most-sponsors.html

Kit sponsorship originated in Uruguay in the 1950s, but it wasn't until 1973 when Jägermeister managed to get its logo on Eintracht Brauschweig's kits that such sponsorship began in earnest.[2] Now, even referees don corporate logos; DEKRA, the largest vehicle inspection company in Germany, graces the upper sleeve of refs in Bundesliga. For all this, however, company avatars and adverts seem to blend in with the spectacle of a football match—much more so than incessant SUV, smartphone, insurance, or US armed forces commercials that interrupt other sports viewing to such a degree one wonders whether it's worth the price of admission.

---

[2]Scott Allen, "A Brief History of Jersey Sponsorship," March 20, 2014. https://www.mentalfloss.com/article/27776/brief-history-jersey-sponsorship.

9 GEISTERSPIEL

On January 25, 2020, I watched FC Bayern demolish FC Schalke, 5-0. This was the cusp of the pandemic. The former were on their way to winning an eighth Bundesliga title in a row; the latter were on their way to finishing twelfth, having two years earlier risen to second place in the league. As usual at the end of the match it wasn't the score that most interested me; it was something that happened before kick-off. Players of both teams and the officiating crew held a banner at mid-field that read #WeRemember. I'd had the TV's sound muted, since my son was already asleep in the adjacent room, so after the match I typed the hashtag into my phone: FC Bayern had been honoring the 75-year anniversary of the liberation of the Auschwitz-Birkenau concentration camp. I rewound the game and watched the moment again: the footballers' appeared deadpan, the 75,000 fans in Allianz Arena were utterly silent, and the announcer was somber. I couldn't help imagining that some of those German players' grandparents or the fans' grandparents had taken part in atrocities. In particular, I thought about superstar forward Robert Lewandowksi, the second-all-time goal scorer for

Bayern and a Polish international footballer: was he thinking about Oświęcim, the Polish name for Auschwitz? Thirty years earlier, I'd visited the concentration camp and the sight of one of the barracks rooms filled with mounds of graying shorn hair has never left me.

On March 11, 2020, I watched a Bundesliga derby between Köln and Mönchengladbach. It was the first pandemic Geisterspiel, "ghost game," the German loanword for matches played without fans in the stands. For a moment I thought back to Auschwitz: all those victims, all those ghosts. The stadium echoed with the voices of coaches and players, including curse words which the broadcasters repeatedly apologized for. You could hear the ball being kicked by each foot. You could hear clapping. And for once, you could hear the communication that I knew existed from my own playing but that you never hear on a broadcast because of fan noise: players talking to each other, guiding each other on the pitch, especially the keeper. Yes, there were benefits to what was missing! That same week I watched a rainy Premier League match made less dreary by the sound of raindrops hitting the roof of the stands.

The pandemic isn't the first time football has experienced fanless or limited fans at matches; to prevent hooliganism stadiums have shuttered their doors before. But the pandemic has certainly been a great threat to the sport, its coverage, its finances. The ad boards still play along the stands, but for only screen watchers. The regular sounds that fill the stadium . . . not everyone will agree with me that they prefer the "natural" sounds of the game over the roars of the crowd. Fans cheering is part of the game. It lifts the spirits not just of the players, but of the fans themselves. Over the months of continued empty stadiums, some broadcasters have elected to pipe in fan noise, others not. And in a few stadiums, artificial fan noise is pumped into the stadium itself so that players, managers, and staff can experience a bit of the old thrill. (When fans return, might there be a tech option to have the players and coaches talk piped into my TV?)

For a moment, let's take the Geisterspiel for what it is: all of us watching from home are the ghosts. On screens we see the game from above, a cock-eyed bird's eye view. The next time you watch a match, first look at the ball, like we all do, and who has it and who is nearby. Then look off the ball, say, at the entire back line or the furthest player from the ball. What's he or she doing? Where are they looking, where does their head turn? When defensive midfielder Xabi Alonso watches a match on TV, he doesn't only follow the ball. "I follow more of the other positions. But the TV cameras are focusing [on the ball], so it isn't very good for the tactical analysis of the game. You need a wider perspective to have a better analysis."[1] That may be next in terms of what new value addition broadcasters can provide at-home viewers. There are simply aspects you can't see via a broadcast: the ground

---

[1] Grant Wahl, *Masters of Modern Soccer: How the World's Best Play the Twenty-First-Century Game* (New York: Crown, 2018), 33.

level or near-ground level shots. (Of course this is one reason to attend a live match.) When you watch players, try homing in on their feet—touches with instep, outside of the boot, and top of the laces. Notice how the feet turn in or out, draw back, follow through, or stop short, and the balance required sometimes on tip-toe as in a dance. Notice how a particular player prefers to take her first touch or trap. As much as shots rocketed on goal are part of the game, so too is subtlety.

If you become bored watching the ball or the players, consider the referee. Aside from pointing out the gaffs they make, it's only relatively recently that football commentators and scholars have examined closely the part that referees play in the sport. In a professional match, there are four officials: the referee, the two line judges, and the "fourth" official who remains on the touchline between the two benches. Watch the referee for just ten minutes, regardless of where the ball is, and see how they must get close to the active play, but also manage to avoid it by shimmying and prancing around players and their passes. These enforcers of rules are also artful in their rule.

I watch professional football matches precisely because I have no emotional attachment to a particular team. I watch for what I might try to mimic in my pickup games: particular skills, like when best to use the backheel pass or how to trap a long ball with the inside of a raised leg opened up and turned out; or, certain tactics, like when the orchestration of an offensive build-up fails, how the players respond to the counterattack. If I'm not watching to imitate, then often

I'm watching in a near mindless state, something like what ecologist and philosopher Timothy Morton calls "stupid meditation." My mind, if not my body, slumps down in front of the TV set and spies the players on the field moving in their "shape" as though they are well-composed schools of fish, the pitch a green sea, the ball a fast-darting black and white speckled minnow. Or not. The best part about watching like a dumb zombie is that metaphors fade away almost as quickly as the mind forms them.

10 PICKUP

What do a plumber, a judge, a preschool teacher, a doctor, an actor, a retiree, a roofer, a college student, a sheriff's deputy, an ex-army grunt, an undocumented migrant, a business professor, a tailor, and a poet all have in common?

Yes, it's being a regular in the weekly game I've played in for the past decade. These are organically formed games, not part of formalized leagues amateur or otherwise, and they exist all over the world. In the States we call them pickup games. In Brazil they're called *pelada* ("naked") and in Trinidad they're called "taking a sweat" (as in working up a sweat). I only know all this because in 2007 Gwendolyn Oxenham and Luke Boughen, ex-college star players, took off in search of "a story that hasn't been told" about these ostensibly trivial games. The couple began their adventures in Trinidad and 20-some-odd countries and three years later completed them in Iran. Along the way, two other friends shot video footage which they shaped into *Pelada*, a 2010 documentary about their experiences.

As I watched the documentary, I realized that Gwen and Luke were enacting precisely what John Turnbull writes about football being a "second language": "[S]occer is played in more or less the same circumstances, by the same rules, around the globe . . . It really requires no translation to be able to play it; it is its own language. It's intuitively understood, you don't need to say anything to be able to play it."[1] As Gwen and Luke navigate the globe, the couple speak bits and pieces of foreign languages, primarily Portuguese and Spanish, but most often we see them engage people simply by holding out the football they carry everywhere and offering a phrase or two about the game in the local language.

One of the most fascinating pickup games they find takes place in Bolivia where they bribe their way into San Pedro Prison, the infamous prison-city in which 3,000 inmates along with many of their families live. With a genuine smile, one of the inmates sums up football in San Pedro: "While we're here, we have nothing. Our life is to play." This could have been equally said by a player in one of the poorest slums in Nairobi, where Gwen and Luke play on Austin's Field, named after an ex-footballer, coach, and activist who cleared the slum's rubbish dump so that he could teach kids to play football. On the obverse side, Gwen and Luke travel to Tokyo where they play at the top of skyscrapers on very expensive pitches where one salaryman speaks for many, "Soccer is the center of my life. I work to save money so I can kick a ball."

---

[1]"Soccer as a Second Language," accessed on December 5, 2020, https://fivebooks.com/best-books/soccer-second-language-john-turnbull/

The range of people Gwen and Luke discover who play pickup games is staggering—from on-call German medics and firefighters playing in uniforms and work boots, to a handful of women herding llamas in the Peruvian Andes, to young Chinese freestylers in a shopping mall in Shanghai. At one point we hear Gwen's voiceover introducing a segment about Arabs and Jews playing in Jerusalem, "There's no way to imagine where the game will take you." She means this literally and metaphorically. By the end of the film, we can read between the lines: the so-called pickup game brings people together if not in a more pure way as compared to the formal academies and pro leagues of the world, then at least in a more organic way—one that allows for a different kind of unexpectedness and, dare one say it, beauty.

After I watch the documentary, I search out Gwen's book, *Finding the Game: Three Years, Twenty-five Countries and the Search for Pickup Soccer*, which details their journey more thoroughly. It's true of the film, but even more so in the book: Gwen is the protagonist. Between Luke and her, she's the one who is more obsessed with the game. She's the one who holds onto the vestige of playing the game at the highest level—and ends up trying out in a combine for the pros in the States (though she doesn't make it). She's the one you are most rooting for. She's also the female half of the couple, and in traveling the world she's the most vulnerable to prejudice, the odds being stacked against her, and her own internal conflicts. In the last pages of her book, Gwen writes about that tryout for the women's team:

Girls wilt my composure, deflate my ego. Playing all the time against guys is a little bit gutless. When I beat out a guy who is faster and stronger than me, I feel good. And when he beats me, I don't dwell on it; he's faster, he's stronger. They're the ones with something to lose, which means I've got the reckless confidence you need to be good.[2]

It might be difficult to big-data crunch how significant pickup games are, not only to those in prison or poverty, but I can vouch for this: during the pandemic both in lockdown and after it was loosened, each of the pandemic players commented variously and continually about the importance of our matches. A core number of players began playing three matches a week, Tuesday and Thursday evenings and Sunday morning. For the first few months, these were smaller matches, 3-a-side or 4-a-side. Often we'd coax our pre-teen or teenage sons and daughters to play if enough of the regulars couldn't come out (my 13-year-old son agreed to play for a month as a 50th birthday present to me). If there were only four of us, we'd play two versus two. Even though the heat index often reached 100-plus degrees throughout summer 2020, we'd play for 90 minutes and sometimes two hours with little more than the briefest pause for a gulp of water. It only seems extreme to me in recollection of what I

---

[2]*Finding the Game*, (New York: St. Martin's Press, 2012), 271.

was on arrival back home: my clothes soaked through with sweat, my toes prune-like as if I'd been swimming, my urine a bright neon yellow the rest of the day. My body may have been utterly spent, but my mind was at ease. Drinking from a can of cold beer in the hot shower after playing felt like the absolute height of civilization.

I thought it might just be me until Tommy said one evening before the game, "I keep telling my partner this is a lot cheaper than the psychiatrist." John, who works in the film industry and had lost 30 pounds after a month of playing, said: "I still love food, but I love this more!" A few weeks later, John began working as a COVID-19 Compliance Officer for WarnerMedia, and would periodically update us on the latest about COVID testing, tracing, and risk assessment. Two Turkish guys saw us playing one day and soon were regular pandemic players. At some point one of them admitted, "I'd not touched a ball in 25 years, even though as a kid we'd play from eight in the morning until midnight. Our mothers couldn't get us in the house." We laughed. He added, "I quit smoking, too, and now I have this—you all." For a month he would also play with his phone in one hand in case he got a call: he was trying to land a deal to make 10 billion boxes of medical-grade gloves for American Health, netting him $237 million dollars. I told him that if it worked out, he'd have to buy us all uniforms. Another player had bought 14,000 two-ounce bottles of hand sanitizer but then couldn't find anyone to re-sell them to. And one player joined us after I recognized him as one of my son's former chess coaches. He was wandering around the edges of our pitch, and I could tell lockdown was not treating him well; he looked piqued, ill. He said he'd lost his job. I beckoned him to join the game. He came the next week and after a month of regular play, I asked how he was doing. "I'm up then I'm down. But out here I can count on soccer to steady me."

11 THE LIFE-CHANGING MAGIC OF THREE-TOUCH

When I turned on the TV for the first match of the Bundesliga after the initial lockdown, I almost expected to see the players six feet apart and using only three touches. This was May 2020. My friends and I had been playing football with three touches for about a month, and no one had shown any outward symptoms of getting sick. At first we named our new system Q-ball (Q for quarantine) or pandemic ball, but neither took. After a while, it was simply three-touch.

On the one hand, three-touch would appear to be a severe limitation: you get only up to three touches on the ball before having to pass or shoot or leave it for the other team . . . four or more touches is essentially a foul. The intention is to prevent a lot of dribbling that would necessitate players getting too close to each other, violating social distance and allowing for possible virus transmission. On the other hand, three-touch is a liberation. Because you get only up to three touches, your teammates have to continually be in a position to support you—meaning to receive a pass in open space. And as soon as you pass one of them the ball, you have to do the same. One might even say three-touch makes the game more fair, even democratic: everyone gets a much higher number of total touches throughout the match. The game suddenly requires total teamwork. If you don't support your teammates, they can't simply try to dribble out of trouble—and your side loses the ball.

At its essence, football is a game of keep-away, and no one is as quick as the ball being passed from player to player. The pass is absolutely crucial, which is why so much of training involves working on it—from the widespread use of the rondo to drills repeating crosses into the box. It's not just the accuracy of the pass, but the "weight" of it: too heavy and the ball overshoots your teammate or is too hard for them to handle; too light and a defender intercepts it.

As a kid, I practiced weighted passes without really knowing it. My sister, two years younger than me but a fabulous athlete, played soccer too, and together we'd practice in the backyard—often punting the ball to each other. Just as often, though, I couldn't get her to play with me, so I made up my own games with the ball. I'd smash it against the garage door and wait for the rebound to practice my traps. Or, I'd juggle the ball and then try to volley it into the basketball hoop in the driveway. But my favorite game was to kick the ball around the outside of the house. Beginning in the front yard, I'd chip the ball over the driveway to the side yard, a precision pass that would have to land within a 10-foot width; then I'd send a pass on the ground between two plums trees on the diagonal, weighted exactly so that the ball would stop before getting to my parents' vegetable garden; next, I'd try another chip shot to get over the corner of the garden's fence so that the ball would land in middle of the backyard; I'd run after the ball, take a few dribbles before sending it around an apple tree, a pear tree, and turning a corner until I reached the edge of the other side yard where my mom had an ornate, if usually overgrown, flower garden; the ball would have to be sent exactly down the middle of the garden along the stone pavers and through the arbor vitae and into the front yard. This made one full loop around the house that I would do over and over, hour upon hour, sometimes reversing direction. Besides making mistakes with the passes—the wrong weight on the ball, inaccuracy, a shanking chip—the biggest problem was to avoid ruining my mom's prized rhododendrons in the front yard. They weren't obstacles, per se, but somehow I almost always managed to snap off a branch or two and would have to hide them in the arbor vitae so that she wouldn't notice. All this is to say that I've never been a fancy dribbler or a striker who can finish in front of the goal, but I realize now that my ability to thread passes to teammates and to distribute the ball quickly and accurately traces back to the "rules" I made up for that childhood game.

Three-touch hasn't only underscored the importance of passing; it's made me realize that dribbling is often obnoxious, unneeded, and not as pretty as I thought it was. Watching a legend like Maradona on the men's side or Marta Vieira da Silva on the women's make their way through three, four, or more defenders is entertaining. But I don't find it as stunning as an offensive build-up composed entirely of one and two-touch passes. About just such a build-up in the 2018 World Cup match between Belgium and Japan, Glen Wilson writes: "Seven touches from end to end, a counter-attack as smooth as it was clinical. Ten seconds and done; the sort of fleeting moment of perfection you invest a lifetime of watching the game for. You could watch it over and over for hours."[1]

What's more, I no longer watch stars such as Messi hoping for him to dribble through the defense or even to make one of his signature left-footed curving shots into the corner of the goal. Instead, I wait for his passes—when he uses his x-ray vision (as Ray Hudson calls it) to pick out a teammate and make a perfectly weighted, seemingly impossible pass.

Hand-in-hand with passing is "vision." Mexican national Chicharito expresses it this way: "You play this sport in the mind, not only on the field. If [your opponent] is more clever than you, you can be faster and stronger, but probably you are not going to beat him. He's one step in front of you in the mind." What he's talking about is predicting power. Some players call it intuition. It's more like lightning-chess than any

---

[1] *WCLDN: London, loneliness, and a long hot football summer* (UK: Cambria, 2020), 96.

other sport I've played. Chicharito talks about the Spanish idiom, "to smell the intuition, to smell [for example] where the cross is going."[2] Some commentators call vision "fluid intelligence" or "spatial reasoning" or "spatial awareness." Most crucial is the pace at which one is able to predict and anticipate scenarios. You'll hear players on the field say "good read" after you've intercepted a pass, especially one that wasn't telegraphed or that no one else really saw in advance; and, you'll hear people say things like "she reads the game well." What these players are reading are *patterns* of play between players and of the behavior of individuals.

Our three-touch matches played three times a week have allowed us to become much better at reading. Particularly in defending against the player with the ball, we read body language: where is the opponent's momentum propelling him, is he leaning to one side, where is his non-kicking foot planted, and depending on the individual, which feints does he usually make, what is his favorite first-touch, and whom does he most like to pass to on his team. Simultaneous to reading an individual opponent, the best players are constantly aware of the positions of as many others on the pitch as possible. All of this is happening in seconds or microseconds.

To improve your reading, you have to increase one specific behavior: turning your head. When I say increase, I mean

---

[2]Grant Wahl, *Masters of Modern Soccer*, 70-71.

continually looking around to see where your teammates and the opposing players are relative to where you are. It's like in baseball before the pitch is thrown: if the ball is hit to me, what should be my first reaction? Three-touch demands, in other words, that you read the pitch continually and that your first touch on the ball is crucial—one that both keeps the ball away from the defender and allows you to pick out a pass or shot with your second and/or third touch. After playing three-touch for months, many of the pandemic players made comments about how our game periodically looked more like a professional game: continual movement off the ball, and continual short passes often in triangles.

My friend Nathan, who grew up in Guatemala, observed us playing one evening. "I figured three-touch was kind of a vague 'rule,'" he said, "but you actually do it. The short, quick passes and movement—it's tiki-taka!"

"The Barça way?"

"And the Spanish national team," he added. "Though we Latin Americans know it was actually a reverse colonization of fútbol, because it had long been the de-facto way of playing in the Americas, except in the US."

I knew what he meant about tiki-taka, the name coined back around 2006 to identify a style of play that is now, at least in part, universal at the top levels. I wanted to add, though, that our three-touch wasn't merely a tactic or a skills exercise, as is sometimes used in training. I needn't have worried. A couple of weeks later Nathan typed up and sent his impressions of our pandemic play:

I see why you say multiple tiki-taka games in the week has replaced the crucial need for yoga or meditation. Tiki-taka quiets the monkey mind because there is no time or space for anything but the present, or the very immediate future: if you don't have the ball, you're always moving to where you can receive it and so is everyone else . . . The time on the pitch is clearly precious to everyone; most of you are middle-aged; when the ball is cleared out of bounds, I'd expected players to walk to get the ball, taking advantage of the opportunity to catch a collective breath; but everyone sprints to get the ball back in play, like kids taking advantage of every second of recess! Every single game offers certain moments, unique, sublime or even ridiculous in their own little way, and I'm sure, based on the joy of this game, that those moments live another life under more than one roof across the city as players lie awake for a few minutes before falling asleep, or perhaps sometimes a flash in the first waking moments of the next day.

12 OF NUTMEGS AND FISH UP A TREE

Only after watching a 1975 New York Cosmos game in which a British broadcaster says his name do I realize that I've been ignoring the accent mark and mispronouncing Pelé my entire life. It's not PE-le, but Pe-LE. Or more precisely, according to my Portuguese-speaking friends, PE-LE, a spondee. But I can't be too hard on myself: almost everyone I know says it incorrectly even though Pelé has been worshipped here for decades. Does that mean we Americans are just ignorant? Yes and no.

I'm thinking of the fact that Henry David Thoreau's last name is always mispronounced: historians tell us that in his time, Thoreau was pronounced like "thorough" and not thur-ROW. I'm thinking of the fact that the rules of language and pronunciation are often in flux. So this past week I asked my students how to pronounce Pelé. Everyone made the same "mistake" as I did and still do. Then, however, one of them asked me to say "crayon." I said KRAN. Most of them laughed. *It's not KRAN, it's KRAY-on.* I reminded them that the little strip of earth between lanes going in different directions on the road is called a "median" everywhere else in the country except in New Orleans where we call it the "neutral ground." This is just one of our city's shibboleths, along with the pronunciations of various street names; in fact, presently when you look up the word "shibboleth" on Wikipedia, the example image is a New Orleans' street name: Tchoupitoulas.

Football, too, has its shibboleths. One can say touchline instead of sideline, or kit instead of uniform, or draw instead of tie, but one had better do it in the proper environs or be prepared for a bit of ridicule or grumbling.

Until I was in college, I thought it was called a "neg"—as in "I just got negged." And I did get negged a lot as a kid playing, probably because I was an old-school fullback, a stopper, not a ball-handler. And if I ever negged anyone else, it was likely an accident. What I mean is *megged*. That's the correct term. To meg, or to use the full term, to nutmeg: to send the ball through the opening between your opponent's legs as a pass, a shot, or on the dribble. To get nutmegged looks and feels embarrassing, and it happens to even the best defensive players, which is why I'm always rankled when another player or a commentator makes a big deal about it. Messi gets megged and the broadcaster will unfurl long sentences about how the player who megged Messi will someday tell his grandchildren about the feat. First, even Messi isn't perfect. Second, Messi is a forward—who cares if he gets megged in the opposing side's half!

What's more interesting is the speculative origins of the term. Does "nut" refer to testicles, and if so, what's the "meg" part about? In *Football Talk: The Language & Folklore of The World's Greatest Game*, Peter Seddon points out a far more likely etymology for nutmeg: that it comes from a duplicitous practice in the nutmeg trade. As he writes, the verb nutmegged is listed by the Oxford English Dictionary as "arising in the 1870s which in Victorian slang came to mean 'to be tricked or deceived, especially in a manner which makes the victim look foolish' . . . Nutmegs were such a valuable commodity that unscrupulous exporters were wont to pull a fast one by mixing a helping of wooden replicas into the sacks being shipped to England." To meg, in short, is to deceive—at least in English.[1] The same feat in other countries has other names. For example, in Austria, it's called *Gurkerl* (little cucumber), and in South Korea, it's called *Alggagi* (알까기) (hatching an egg).

Football seems to revel in its idiomatic usages, especially in how players communicate with each other on the pitch. If you don't play the game, you might not be familiar with terms like touch, backdoor, line, square, overlap, switch, trailer, drop, cross, cut back, mark up, contain, time, leave, turn, to feet, lay off, close down, hold, clear, dummy, and man on. This last one has confounded me when I've coached girls youth soccer, or during our pandemic play when women are

---

[1] *Football Talk*, 113-14.

on the pitch or when the daughter of one of the players, who's 11 years old and plays at least twice a week with us, is about to tackle a teammate; sometimes I yell "man on" to warn my teammate and sometimes I yell "girl on." Neither sounds right. In other locales, for example, there are other words or phrases to indicate that pressure is coming: in Brazil players yell *ladrão* (thief); in Portugal they yell *polícia* (cop); and, in the Netherlands they yell *in je rug* (in your back).

Even if one has played for years, there still seem to be idioms to glean. In my football watching mania, I've learned a number of new terms and phrases from British commentators. *Asking questions of the defense. Do they have an answer?* That's the way they talk about an offensive challenge that might include a fine build-up down one of the flanks or a cross that leads to a shot. (As a poet, I might identify this Q & A as "call and response.") In American English, we'd use "chance" or "opportunity": *so-and-so created a good opportunity for so-and-so in the box.* Two other British usages come up again and again: "cynical" to describe a foul that was unwarranted or malicious, and "clinical" to describe a clean and efficient "finish" (i.e. goal). *That was a cynical attempt at a foul, but she avoided it and was clinical in her finishing.*

More than any particular Britishism, however, there is a British commentator whose linguistic festooning continues to attract my attention—that of Ray Hudson, analyst for beIN Sports. Hudson joined Newcastle United at age 17, moved to the States a few years later to play in the North

American Soccer League for the Fort Lauderdale Strikers, and eventually coached two MLS teams in the early 2000s. Then for three years he cleaned pools before getting his first job in broadcasting. Today he is best-known for narrating La Liga matches, particularly for Barcelona and Real Madrid, from Florida via the wonders of satellite technology. If you've not watched his broadcasts, there's a Twitter handle where a fan documents Hudson's linguistic gymnastics: @liverayhudson. To read the feed is the opposite of doom-scrolling. Hudson mimics the inventiveness of the play on the pitch with the inventiveness of his language:

Benzema's going to pounce on that pass like Dracula on a plate of liver.

Ramos rises in the air like a fresh salmon from a summer stream to head it in.

The defence goes missing like the kids in *The Blair Witch Project*.

The touch of this free kick: soft as a slug's beer belly and sweeter than the moonlight through the pines.

A fish up a tree finish, but applaudable in its failure.

While observers have pointed out that Hudson's figurations are reminiscent of darts commentator Sid Waddell's ("Even Hypotenuse would have trouble working out these angles!"),

Hudson so far outstrips the comparison that I have difficulty choosing which elaborations to cite:

> Pretty, pretty goal. Should be on the back of a truck's mudflap. Wonderful vision, great execution, and he doesn't just beat Asenjo, he Hannibal Lecters him. Terminates with extreme prejudice.

> He's handing out chocolates to the defenders as he goes by. Slippery as an ice cube on the top of an oven. The defenders can't contain him & we can't comprehend him. More twists and turns than a cheap garden hose.

> What a goal by Kroos. It's the type of finish, Phil, you could hang up in the Louvre, as a work of art of how to finish . . . painted like a Seurat dot. Magical.

> The azimuth angles, the minutes, the degrees: [Messi] takes the planets into alignment and consideration with the gravitational pull of this ball. That Stradivarius of a left foot. Again, man, centipedes go to sleep at night and dream of just having one left foot like his!

> Hotter than the hinges of hell's gate, Lionel here, as he steps up and caresses this one where the spiders live . . . He takes the goalkeeper, the defender on the line into account, and probably the rings of Saturn, too.

Some viewers can't stand this kind baroque verbiage. Others love it. What probably helps keep it all in check is his co-

commentator, Phil Schoen, who provides the straightforward play-by-play, a foil to Hudson's bombasticity. Schoen also takes verbal licks from Hudson without offense, and often they spar amiably, which seems to be part of their success; the duo has been announcing games together for more than 15 years. Moreover, when you watch a Real Madrid or Barcelona match on a day when Hudson is absent, you realize how lackluster the substitute commentator is. The substitute may be a more insightful "expert" on the players or the tactics, but the color fades. As with Howard Cosell (boxing, Monday Night Football) or Harry Carey (Chicago Cubs baseball) or Peggy Fleming (figure skating), you get not just an announcer but a personality with Hudson, a character who gives you another layer of entertainment accompanying the one you are watching. And even if you know many of his linguistic tics, you never know exactly what he'll say— his language becomes as much a part of the experience of watching football as the football itself is.

13 FOR THE LOVE OF A PRETTY MOVE

While some fans more than others may enjoy the language of the game, everyone enjoys witnessing beautiful play—whether it occurs at the professional level or in a backyard, street, or park. In *Football in Sun and Shadow*, Eduardo Galeano makes an early confession: "I go about the world, hand outstretched, and in stadiums I plead: 'A pretty move, for the love of God.'" I would like to argue that it's not just the prettiness we're attracted to; it's the difference and distance between what we expect to see and what we see. A certain degree of unpredictability is at the heart of football's beauty.

At the top of the list are moves, tricks, feints, or any number of other labels that refer to the same thing: deception.[1] With

---

[1] I do not mean the wondrous stunts footballers have done with the ball, like Maradonna blasting a ball 25 meters straight up into the air, waiting for it to come down, blasting it again the same way, and repeating the feat 13 times without moving more than a few meters in any direction; or, Ronaldinho juggling a ball at the top of the box, then suddenly smash-volleying it off the

a certain movement or series of movements, the player with the ball tries to deceive their opponent(s) in order to pass, shoot, dribble around, or otherwise gain advantage. Footballers have invented dozens of tricks, and many of them are named after their creators: the Puskas V move, the Cruyff turn, the Maradona, etc. In his autobiography, *I Am Zlatan*, the Swedish footballer Zlatan Ibrahimović talks about learning tricks from Ronaldo and other Brazilians by watching videos: "We were all used to touching the ball. But the Brazilians would sort of nudge it with their foot, and we'd practice over and over again until the thing worked . . . I went deeper into it. I was more precise in the details. I became completely obsessed." The whole concept of feints is a tactic of play, but it's also something else: a means of getting individual attention. For Zlatan, an outsider, an immigrant kid from a ghetto in Malmö, feints became central to his identity: "[P]eople were just excited about my tricks and fancy moves, and it got me going . . . I felt bigger when people recognized me."[2] Recognition is at the heart of identity, but what any player, or any person for that matter, wants is to be appreciated. Zlatan pushed his notorious style of play

---

crossbar, the ball coming right back to him still in the air, his controlling it effortlessly, juggling it a few more times, and then repeating the shot off the crossbar and subsequent control and juggle and another shot and another—four times with the ball never touching the ground.

[2]Zlatan Ibrahimović (with David Lagercrantz), *I Am Zlatan: My Story on and Off the Field* (New York: Random House, 2011), 66.

augmenting it with comments to the media after the match: "First I went left, and he [defender Stéphane Henchо] did too. Then I went right, and he did too. Then I headed left, and he went out to buy a hot dog."[3] The wow-factor of tricks are rarely enough, however, as Zlatan admitted after signing his first huge contract ($10 million) at age 19: [M]y moves . . . weren't necessarily appreciated at Ajax unless they led to something concrete."[4]

The most concrete aspect of football are the goals—or the lack of them. In fact, if you want to see "just the goals," there's a film series for that: FIFA's "All the Goals" is described as "a football feast for fans who just love to see the ball in the back of the net. Just sit back, press play and enjoy." I admit I took the bait and watched all 120 minutes worth of goals for the 2006 World Cup held in Germany. Initial problem: they show the final score of the game before showing the goals, which is something like telling you how a novel ends on the first page. On the plus side, they often show the build-up to each goal and not simply the final blast or tap in. While I sat and watched each of the goals, not getting up once for a snack or to use the bathroom, there was something thoroughly unsatisfying about watching goal after goal.

Entire chapters and books are devoted to the subject of goals. In *The Numbers Game: Why Everything You Know about*

---

[3]Ibid, 109.
[4]Ibid.

Soccer is Wrong, Chris Anderson and David Sally put forth a number of times the same declaration: soccer is the goal, and the goal is soccer. Everything depends on scoring—the game's winners and losers, of course, but more importantly the game's beauty. Then, the authors break down, quite well and in enough detail for you to go along with the book's overall thrust, all the big data about the game. Their most pronounced conclusion is that soccer at the highest level—the top five flights of Europe—is homogeneous. They're correct if one considers how globalization and profit motives have heightened the pace, skill level, and tactics of the game to an unprecedented level—a level that can plateau. The variation between players and teams is often "cosmetic," as they point out.

But it's the part about goals being the goal of football that continually troubles me. The goal, to me, is not the goal, not the scoring, or even the winning. The goal of soccer is no goal. The beauty of the game is in its very play—its ongoingness of play, whether I'm watching it live, recorded, or playing it. It is about the series of moment-to-moments—the patterns and variations. If you want the "artist" conceptualization, this means process over product. And for the product to mean more than simply a box score there should be a specific measure of "chance and drama" for fans. At least according to Nicholas Christenfeld, a psychologist who has studied the "optimal level of chaos" in sports:

There must be some balance of skill and chance in a sport's outcome to create both meaning and suspense, and, thereby, pleasure. Based on a comparison of multiple sports, there is reason to think that the best blend is actually quite specific . . . Sports can tune their blend of skill and chance in all sorts of ways. They can, as the NBA does, impose salary caps, which homogenize talent and make luck more potent . . . Sports can also allow minor differences in behavior to have a major impact on outcomes.[5]

In football, one of these minor differences would be the offside rule, a difference that can be so slight that even in video replays it can be all but impossible to discern whether a player is in an offside position or not.[6] And yet, offside calls have determined many a goal and a game.

Those who find soccer boring aren't necessarily wrong; they are simply not used to the patterns of chance in the game.[7] High scores don't always equal excitement in a sport.

---

[5]"What do good sports and great romances have in common? An optimal level of chaos." The Washington Post, March 15, 2016. https://www.washingtonpost.com/news/in-theory/wp/2016/03/15/how-to-keep-sports-interesting/

[6]In the States, you will most often hear "offsides" not "offside"; I think of it as a minor irritation like the UK's "maths" vs. the US's "math."

[7]Neuroscientist Alex Korb argues that watching soccer releases dopamine in the brain, similar to how sex does, and that if viewers haven't watched enough soccer, "They don't have enough soccer experience to read the cues, so their brains don't release dopamine for all these little situations. They're just waiting for a goal, and those rarely–and sometimes never–happen.

Consider basketball: a 110-89 game might be entirely dull as compared to an 89-87. In soccer, what's the analogue situation? A 0-0 match (an often occurrence) but one in which defenses have stymied offensive players numerous times, or offensive players have had plenty of solid shots on goal but none met the back of the net. Boredom, in other words, isn't necessarily or directly linked to goals, though it's been perceived that way many times.

Before the US hosted the 1994 World Cup, FIFA allowed for "test matches," tinkering with some of the sport's parameters—a 30-yard offside line, a no offside rule, larger goals—in a failed attempt to increase the number of goals in a match. Then, in 1996, before it was set to play its first season, MLS queried FIFA again about enlarging the size of the goal (18 inches wider and 9 inches taller) to "stimulate scoring"; FIFA summarily rejected the idea as well as another about the size of the ball.[8]

But who knows how conventions of the game may change? A few years ago it was reported that FIFA is considering "run-up" shootouts for the 2026 World Cup matches

---

So yes, for them, soccer is boring." "Sex, Dopamine and the World Cup," *Psychology Today*, June 30, 2014. https://www.psychologytoday.com/us/blog/prefrontal-nudity/201406/sex-dopamine-and-the-world-cup

[8]Grahame L. Jones, "Goal Size to Remain the Same, FIFA Rules," *LA Times*, March 10, 1996. https://www.latimes.com/archives/la-xpm-1996-03-10-sp-45390-story.html

that end in a draw at regulation time.[9] These would look something like the shoot-out I remember practicing and taking part in in the mid-1980s: from about 30-35 yards out, a player would face the opposing goalie, charging forward in a hard dribble then shooting for goal. It felt like a solo break-away against the goalie, and was much more entertaining than the conventional penalty kick from the spot. Even when one would miss, there was the thrill of the goalie stopping the shot. Ultimately, it's not that a goal is beautiful in and of itself. Some are more beautiful than others, of course (cf. a deflection off a defender versus a dipping strike over a five-defender wall from a set-piece). The goals that do not materialize—the blast off a post or the crossbar—can be equally beautiful for how close they come.

On the flipside, what about the goals prevented? When one of the pandemic players asked Rodolfo, one of the best "finishers" among us, how many goals he scored at the end of a Sunday match, he humbly admitted "three or four." Jimmy overheard the exchange, then added, "That's great. But ask me how many goals I stopped." It was a good point. Jimmy is notorious for shutting down an offensive attack, even a one on three or four situation. While we entertain the general

---

[9]Caitlin Murray, "FIFA Considers Run-up Shootouts for 2026 World Cup like MLS Used in the 1990s." https://www.foxsports.com/stories/soccer/fifa-considers-run-up-shootouts-for-2026-world-cup-like-mls-used-in-the-1990s

notion that "the best offense is a good defense," we still data-crunch goals and attempts-on-frame with little regard for tracking snuffed out goals. What does this say about measuring performance, measuring winning? *Did you score? Did you at least get an assist?*

A goal doesn't come out of nowhere. It begins with a defensive move. And a goal that comes from a "counter attack" (don't they all, in essence?) usually does no justice to its origins. The fact is, in our pickup games many of us are almost always oblivious about the score. Instead, we are focused on one thing: the play we are in or the one we are on the verge of. These are at once continuous moments and fleeting ones, and if there is a "goal," it's that we try to experience these moments as many times as possible in the course of two hours.

14 ZONE

In spring 2020, German goalkeeper Marc-André ter Stegen shared his thoughts about life under quarantine: "People have always laughed when I have told them I have no idea about football. This is because I don't watch a lot of football, only when there are big games on or when there's a match that's of interest to me because I have a friend involved. But I really miss the smell of the grass."[1]

This is both surprising (one of the best keepers in the game doesn't watch football?) and illuminating. It's not just that ter Stegen loves to play the game instead of observe it, it's what he's intimating: that he loves *to be* in the game—experiencing every aspect, including the "smell of the grass." My cohorts and I have talked about this for years: while we are playing the game nothing else exists including and perhaps especially a sense of self. That "flow" that people talk

---

[1]"Barça goalie ter Stegen's coronavirus diary," ESPN. https://www.espn.com /soccer/barcelona/story/4092109/barca-goalie-ter-stegens-coronavirus-d iary-keeping-fitkeeping-sane-and-bonding-with-family-at-home

about when watching pro footballers move as schools of fish isn't just something to witness from a distance. It's there on the inside of players. "Being in the zone" is the phrase athletes as well as musicians will use to describe the phenomenon. The zone is a place where you are part of something large (spatially) but also so deeply invested into the present moment (time-bound), such that you feel utterly at ease and heightened simultaneously. It's a special kind of bliss, to me, that is unique as compared to that of, say, having sex.

If you focus too much on being in the zone, however, you're soon taken out of it. "Don't overthink it," players and coaches admonish young players, implying that too much self-awareness can be a liability. The key phrase is "too much" because you still have to be very aware of your position on the pitch relative to everyone else's. The zone feeling can also be accompanied by an almost Eliotesque time present/time future experience. In his memoir, Boston Celtics basketball legend Bill Russell writes: "It was almost as if we were playing in slow motion. During those spells I could almost sense how the next play would develop and where the next shot would be taken."

When a player says that she isn't really thinking when she's playing or that it's all "very natural," it's because the patterns of thought-cum-action are incredibly well-worn. The hard thinking, and the muscle memory of doing a task such as trapping or passing with the instep, has already happened innumerable times long before. The psychologist Mihaly Csikszentmihalyi, an original researcher on the concept of "flow," describes the zone as follows: "There's this focus that, once it becomes intense, leads to a sense of ecstasy, a sense of clarity: you know exactly what you want to do from one moment to the other . . . time disappears. You forget yourself. You feel part of something larger." Time goes away—or maybe it just compresses—and thus people talk about adults becoming children again when they play football. The zone or "pure" play that children may experience, however, is different from organized sports. Csikszentmihalyi argues that the zone occurs when there is an equal balance of skill and challenge, and that inside the zone is where our greatest moments of happiness are.[2] Philosopher Heather Reid adds that,

Enhancing one's performance with drugs, focusing on victory, and pursuing external goods do not produce more enjoyment in sport or more frequent experiences of the zone. If anything, they interfere with these play-like benefits. The autotelic value [the value of doing an activity for its own sake] of sport, it turns out, depends on training and competing the old fashioned way."[3]

---

[2]Mihaly Csikszentmihalyi. "Flow, the secret of happiness." *TED: Ideas Worth Spreading*, February 2004. https://www.ted.com/talks/mihaly_csikszentmih alyi_flow_the_secret_to_happiness

[3]Reid, Heather, *Introduction to the Philosophy of Sport* (Lanham, MD: Rowman & Littlefield, 2012). Kindle Edition.

The combination of skill, challenge, and training is a type of zone I know from creative activities—writing poems where the mind is fully engaged in wordplay or character and story, or painting where the mind is focused solely on the materiality of paint and canvas, color and shape and line. I can feel a certain ecstasy in being in this creative zone, but both activities are relatively sedentary endeavors. Only when I'm in the middle of playing football, because of its pace and the addition of constant movement, are my mind and body thoroughly and hyperly present at once. What's curious to those observing this state from the outside is that it doesn't look "happy," it looks *boring*—the player allegedly engaged in the zone displays a glazed over countenance, appearing almost indifferent.

Almost. Because if you want to take in the experience without actually playing the game, track down *Zidane, un portrait du 21e siècle* (*Zidane: A 21*st *Century Portrait*), a 2006 film documentary that follows the French footballer Zinedine Zidane for one entire match—17 cameras focused exclusively on him.[4]

---

[4]The documentary is difficult to find, at least in the States: I had to order a bootleg copy on DVD from France.

15 A 21ST CENTURY PORTRAIT

Zidane was famous long before he head-butted Marco Materazzi in the 110th minute of the 2006 World Cup Final, and was summarily red-carded and sent off. This was Zidane's last match as a professional footballer. People called his final act "lunacy" and that's what my wife and I thought as we watched the TV broadcast in a friend's apartment near the Eiffel Tower.[1] Neither of us really cared

---

[1]For Materazzi's part, he declared, "Yes, I was tugging his [Zidane's] shirt, but when he said to me scornfully 'If you want my shirt so much I'll give it to you afterwards' is that not a provocation? I answered that I'd prefer his sister, it's true . . . It's not a particularly nice thing to say, I recognize that. But loads of players say worse things . . . I didn't even know he had a sister before all this happened." Both Materazzi and Zidane were given game suspensions, but because Zidane had retired from football he was made to do three days of community service instead. Materazzi would later go on to publish a book about the head-butt incident because as he states, "[E]veryone asked me what I had told him to react like that. My words were stupid but did not deserve that reaction." Apparently, Materazzi wanted to clarify a few things, such as, "I talked about his sister not his mother, like I have read in some

who won the final and although I knew Zidane was a star, I'd not followed him or much of football for years. As soon as Italy won, beating France on penalty kicks, the entire city of Paris went silent. Even the next morning, a lovely July day, Parisians and tourists seemed reticent in the markets and at the cafes.

Recently, I sought out the video clip of the head-butt and watched it a dozen times. It's not nothing. But 15 years on, Zidane has done much more. As manager of Real Madrid, where he previously was a star player, he's known for taking a hands-on, one-on-one approach with his players—working overtime to develop each of them. As of the beginning of the 2020-21 season, the record shows he's won an impressive 11 titles for the club in his two stints as manager. But as any manager of the top flight clubs, he's been lauded and derided, if not in equal measure, then at least by twists, turns, and entanglements. To me, none of this is as intriguing as the film documentary about Zidane in a La Liga fixture that occurred the year before his retirement. The date: April 23, 2005 (Shakespeare's 441st birthday). The match: Real Madrid

---

newspapers. My mother died while I was a teenager, I would never insult his." https://www.sportsjoe.ie/football/marco-materazzi-finally-confirms -said-zinedine-zidane-86443 https://www.theguardian.com/football/2006/ sep/05/newsstory.sport15

Zidane's act prompted a range of contentious works, including the pamphlet *La mélancolie de Zidane* by Jean-Philippe Toussaint and the sculpture *Coup de tête* by Adel Abdessemed.

vs. Villarreal, before 80,000 fans at the Santiago Bernabéu, Real's home stadium.

As the documentary opens I keep thinking about its title. Is this going to be "21st century" simply because the match takes place in 2005? What specifically will be "of this century" about the film, or of Zidane? That his post-colonial Algerian heritage is emblematic of so many other players in today's game? That new technology allows for high-definition camera work, capturing the intricacies of play? Whatever it is, the video, on the 20th century technology of my 20-year old DVD player, initially looks like an art-house film, with the appropriate art-house type electronic background music of Mogwai. That's not a dig. I like Mogwai. I like art-house films.

Instead of following the ball (our usual focus of watching), the premise of the documentary is to follow a single player for an entire match. Immediately, we get close-ups of Zidane in his attacking midfielder role. We see his facial reactions after a pass—the concentrated look, the stoicism. At times the close-ups are so close one can see the pores on his nose and cheeks, the individual whiskers of his Don Johnson facial stubble, and, as the match wears on, the droplets of perspiration falling from his forehead, chin, and nose.

Then something begins to dominate our attention: the sheer amount of walking that Zidane is doing. How often and to what extent do we pay attention to *walking* of all things on the pitch, even by a player of the highest caliber?

This becomes anti-dramatic or anti-narrative. One watches continual moments of "unimportance": Zidane's loping, at times hop-skipping while dragging his toe against the pitch, a kind of tick; then his repositioning and looking around, presumably for moments of "importance" like a tremendous pass or shot. In fact, the predominant camera shot is of Zidane from the mid-thigh or knee down, walking between occasional sprints for the ball or to an open space. At first I think that his thighs and knees are not particularly stellar to look upon, very unlike, say, the hot thighs of Cristiano Ronaldo which we see every time Ronaldo pulls up his shorts in preparation to take a free kick, as though, in the words of Glen Wilson "he's about to wade through a deep river."[2] But after a while, I begin to prefer Zidane's knobby knees and hairy thighs.

The film includes no narration besides the crowd and field sounds and the occasional intercut to the live La Liga broadcast in Spanish, often in replay after a foul on or by Zidane. During an intense moment of play, the cheers of the fans are turned up or down for a bit of dramatic emphasis. More subtly, we also hear the swish of his shorts, his breath increasing as he sprints down the pitch, and the satisfying thump on the grass when he goes down after being lightly tackled.

---

[2] Glen Wilson, *WCLDN: London, loneliness, and a long hot football summer*, 89.

What will be quite new to many at-home viewers are the ground-level shots—the vision that a player has on the field, the one I miss most when I watch a broadcasted game. Different aspects literally come into view; for example, the dozens of camera flashes that pop out from the stands when Zidane has the ball, especially near a sideline. There's one particular arty shot in slow-motion, zoomed-in on Zidane's boots as he walks—all other sound omitted, only that of a boot sinking into sod. It's tender, melodic, as though we're following someone's steps as they traipse a grassy path right after a spring rain.

The first attempt at any kind of dramatic arc happens around the 22-minute mark: accompanied by ambient electronic music, Zidane "speaks" in subtitles about how, as a kid, there ran a commentary in his head as he played. It wasn't his voice, he says, it was the voice of Pierre Cangioni, a 1970s broadcaster who announced games: "Every time I heard his voice, I would run towards the TV. As close as I could get. For as long as I could. It wasn't that his words were so important. But the tone, the accent, the atmosphere, was everything." Then, as the music crescendos, comes a scene of Zidane taking a spill and getting right back up. He grunts— one of the only times we actually hear Zidane's voice in the match, other than when he says, *ahí, ahí* (there, there) asking for a teammate to pass to him in space.

At halftime, the score is Real Madrid 0, Villarreal 1. Instead of the 15 minutes of commercials or commentary that we would normally view in between halves, there's a montage of what happened outside of the stadium on April 23, 2005—ranging from a car bomb explosion in Iraq, to Voyager 1's entering the solar system's final frontier, to the first sighting of an ivory-billed woodpecker in North America since 1920. The sequence closes with the words "an ordinary day like this might be forgotten." (When I look up the date myself, I also discover that the first YouTube video was uploaded on the same day.)

The second half looks very similar to the first—though Zidane perspires more. I realize that his game looks more workaday than anything else. It's a game and it's a job. At least that's what I read from his countenance: no smiles, no downturned lips, no raised eyebrows.[3] There are periodic loogies and nose-blows. I know them, but I don't get paid for them. But there are expectations around Zidane, as well as the lesser known players, not just to play, but to entertain—to win with panache. Zidane ultimately fulfills this promise: he makes a lovely dribble down the left side of the box, with stepovers and feints, and then sends a left-footed cross to Ronaldo (Brazilian Ronaldo) who heads the ball exceptionally, if easily, into the net. Minutes later something happens—one can't quite tell what—and suddenly Zidane finally reveals emotion: he beams a

---

[3]Film critic Peter Bradshaw not inappropriately calls the look on Zidane's face "as gaunt as an Easter Island statue." https://www.theguardian.com/film/2006/sep/29/documentary

smile at Ronaldo—a big, if garish, genuine smile for a long moment. Less than two minutes later, there's a brawl. We see Zidane rush over and get in the middle of it; he earns a red card. As he walks off the field, he displays the same unnerved expression and body language that he will do a year hence—in the World Cup final—after his head-butting the chest of Materazzi.

A question: If we shot 10, 20, or 100 games that focused solely on Zidane, would we witness something other than what we do in this particular match? Would we see certain patterns of play, of style, of the Zidane "system" over the course of games and seasons? These kinds of algorithm-seeking questions are the biggest reason big data is now with us. The documentary, however, isn't interested in data. Zidane's subtitled voice-overs make this clear: "My memories of games and events are fragments. When you are immersed in the game, you don't really hear the crowd, you can almost decide for yourself what you want to hear. You are never alone. I can hear someone shift around in their chair. I can hear someone coughing. I can hear someone whisper in the ear of someone else." You may have to be in the right frame of mind, and you may have to still be playing the game regularly, to be brought to near-tears by what the film tries to access through Zidane: the phenomenon of being on the pitch in the heart of play where there's nothing but fluid movement in space, and your mind is so attuned to details and focused as to obliviate all else. It is as sublime a feeling as I've ever experienced, and yet at the same time it's also exactly what Zidane says in voice-over in the film's final moment: "Magic is sometimes close to nothing at all."[4]

[4]The Zidane documentary is predated by a German documentary, *Fußball wie noch nie* (*Football as Never Before*) about Manchester United footballer George Best. Eight cameras followed Best in a match against Coventry City on September 12, 1970. The filmmaker, Hellmuth Costard, was something of a renegade; two years earlier he made a brief film, *Besonders wertvoll* (*Of Special Merit*), that featured a penis reciting a new German morality cinema law while being jerked off by a female hand. The Zidane documentary also influenced Spike Lee's *Kobe Doin Work*, which in similar fashion tracks Kobe Bryant for one entire game (April 13, 2008).

16 ZONE PAINTING

When the famed ex-Arsenal manager Arsène Wenger talks about the psychological profile of young players and how by age 20, 67% of them stop playing football altogether, he emphasizes the stamina of a player's mindset.[1] It is not necessarily the most talented player, but the one who can mentally work through frustrations, disappointments, and failures, who keeps progressing in football. This is similar to any number of activities and disciplines, sports or otherwise, that we may often begin as a child or teenager. It's not chiefly about talent, it's about the ability to endure, with or without encouragement. It is my own experience in becoming a poet and writer—the years of rejections, going unpublished, the training, the hundreds, then thousands, of pages of awful or near awful writing. Endurance can pattern up like a good or bad habit, and at some point you have to admit there's either a plan B or not.

One moment of backhanded motivation sticks out. When I was a grad student in creative writing at the University of Memphis, I decided to take an undergraduate Painting

---

[1] A running thread throughout his memoir, *Wenger: My Life and Lessons in Red and White* (San Francisco: Chronicle, 2020).

I course. The professor's father, a noted painter and former professor at the university who at 80 was still painting 12 hours a day, visited our studio. He walked around during critique, offering bits of advice here and there until at the end of class he asked us to look at each other. We sort of did. "No," he said, "really turn to one another and *look*." We complied. "There are 12 of you in the room. Eight won't be painting six months from now, 10 won't be in a year. And maybe one in two years. Most likely none of you will be painters." I felt my stomach drop, not because I wanted to be a painter, but because I wanted to be a poet and what he said, I intuitively knew, applied to writing poems as well. Then he said, "Don't feel bad about this. Nobody said you had to or should be a painter. It's just something you want at the moment." I don't see either wanting to play the game of football, as our 13-year-old son does, or even being a fan of football right now, as being any different. It's something one wants to do presently but that may not always be the case. One's interest may rise or fall, and one will endure that, too.

The funny thing is, I still paint. It's one of my go-to self-medications. When lockdown put an end to playing or watching football, I dragged the box of tubes of paint and brushes out of the attic and ordered canvases. Over the weeks I painted whenever I could slip away from the household chaos, and if that was too tricky, then virus-panic driven insomnia would get me up in the dead of night for a three-hour painting session. For whatever reason, I began doing stained glass images layered in thick paint, over and over, leaving five to 10 underpaintings. Knowing that I was also working on a book about football, my painter-friend Joel saw the new work and made the connection, "Have you forgotten about my hero de Staël? His paintings of soccer players!"

The story goes that on the evening of March 26, 1952, Nicolas de Staël went to see France play Sweden at the Parc des Princes stadium in Paris. He was so enraptured by the experience that afterwards he went straight home and began sketches for *Les Footballeurs*, a series of 24 paintings that would become his most acclaimed.[2] The match was the first ever held under floodlights in France, and the flashes of color from the players' kits against the night backdrop were especially striking.[3]

[2]The largest of the series, *Parc des Princes*, (79" x 138") was kept in the de Staël family until 2019 when it sold for 20 million Euros.
[3]Photograph from *Le Miroir des sports*, No. 343, 31 March 1952. Courtesy of Presse Sports.

Two weeks after the match, he wrote to his friend, the poet René Char:

> When you come back we will go and watch some games together. They are marvellous. No one there is playing to win, except in rare moments of nervousness which cut you to the quick. On the red or blue field, between earth and sky, a ton of muscle flies in abandon, forgetting themselves entirely in the paradoxical concentration that this requires. What joy René, what joy![4]

What de Staël discerned through his painter's eye was the state of being in the zone. In fact, I believe it's because de Staël was a painter—and knew very well an analogous zone in the making of his own work—that the football experience resonated so strongly with him. He was primed for it, in particular, because his style troubled the line between abstract and figurative painting, always trying both to capture the moment of representation (in this case, footballers in a live game) and the moment of setting down paint on a surface. If you take a look at the paintings,

---

[4]Nicolas de Staël, "Letter to René Char, 10 April 1952," cited in: Françoise de Staël, Ed., *Nicolas de Staël: Catalogue Raisonné de l'Oeuvre Peint* (Neuchâtel, 1997), 975. https://www.christies.com/lotfinder/Lot/nicolas-de-stael-1914 -1955-les-footballeurs-parc-6191977-details.aspx

even online, you will notice his trademark thick layers of paint, done with palette knife and trowel instead of brush, that display the zone itself. In a very tangible way, *Les Footballeurs* is the painting equivalent of not just observing football, but playing it.

17 FUTURE STRONGER IN COLOR[1]

I play with men and women (far fewer in number) whose ages range from 13 to 68. Leaving out the occasional pre-teen, the mean age on any given day might be 30 or 40 or 45. It's not uncommon for a few languages besides English to be spoken on the pitch—Spanish, French, Turkish—and over the years regulars have come from all over the world, at least originally. Hans from Holland, Matthias from Germany, Rodolfo from Mozambique, Meno from Belize, Roman from Jamaica, Mikey from Nigeria, Oz from Peru, Nanou from France, Craig from Ireland, Fouad from Morocco, Alex from Wales, Juan from Uruguay, Cihan from Turkey, Gonzalo from Spain, Wesley from Puerto Rico and on and on. This reflects the local situation—our cosmopolitan city—as well as what one sees today in many of the top leagues of the world, especially in Europe. It can still be striking, however,

---

[1] I borrow the title of this chapter from the name of designer Prabal Gurung's fashion collection propelling diversity and inclusion in the industry.

to turn on a Premier League match and notice that nine out of the starting 11 players are not from England. To me, such diversity may be the most beautiful part of the game.

While there are now more players of color on the pitch, are there more people of color in the stands? In summer 2020, as so many matches went into Geisterspiel-mode, Rory Smith recalled an important lesson about diversity from the Premier League's first year. In 1992, at Highbury, Arsenal's stadium, an immense canvas mural depicting fans was put up on one end of the pitch to hide construction work. The day before the first match of the season, Kevin Campbell, a Black Arsenal player, pointed out that no one who looked like him was in the mural: all the fans were White. To the club's credit, the mural was changed overnight so that for the opening match people of color were now in the stands.[2] Women and children, however, were still absent.

A number of terms come to mind to identify what this event highlights: institutional and systemic racism, and implicit bias. Underlying each is the default pattern of so many societies: White and male. And because it is the default or "standard" it can go unnoticed not only by those who are White and male but even by some who are BIPOC. In the above case, when Campbell had first asked another

---

[2]Rory Smith tells a much fuller story in "The Shirts Were Red. The Fans Were All White," *The New York Times*, June 20, 2020. https://www.nytimes.com/2020/06/08/sports/soccer/arsenal-north-bank-mural.html

Black teammate if he saw anything odd about the mural, his teammate failed to notice any problems. The prejudiced patterns of society are so ingrained that people can fail to recognize them unless they are explicitly pointed out—and even then there is often hesitation. But for those who are marginalized, there is continual subjection to an insidious kind of self-awareness: that almost everything is stacked against you.

This applies even if some facets of stereotypes are "positive." I've lost count of how many times commentators and critics default to pat ideas and phrases for groups of players, tagged by race or by country. One of the most recurring is a traditional British kind of "rough, physical" play versus a Brazilian play called *joga bonito* (literally "play beautifully"). Each time I hear or read, for example, that "all Brazilians are amazing dribblers," I become uneasy. I've played with many Brazilians who've had an excellent touch. But when I have witnessed a very fine move or had to try to stop a dazzling run, my immediate thought has been: *My god, he must've practiced that move thousands of times.* In *Football Against the Enemy*, Simon Kuper often expresses similar thoughts about stereotyping; here about Cameroon footballers in the 1990s:

> I discovered why Cameroonians are good at football; they play a lot. Forget all that nonsense about African suppleness . . . at lunchtime, in the evening, and all weekend, Yaoundé [the capital], turns into a football pitch

. . . the quality of play is rare . . . close control was perfect
. . . total football on show . . . a scout would have run out
of notebook.[3]

For the sake of argument, let's say that a fair number of
Brazilian footballers are very good ball-handlers because
of the patterns of play propelled in Brazil. Are all great
dribblers therefore Brazilian? The problem is not just that
the stereotype is often employed to make a specific point, an
expedient certainly not limited to football, but also that the
stereotype propels more stereotyped thinking. In the early
1970s, psychologists Amos Tversky and Daniel Kahneman
proposed the "representativeness heuristic" to identify how
people make quick judgements based on categorical, i.e.,
stereotyped, thinking: because human activity is complex,
and increasingly faster, they began to demonstrate how
cognitive biases (mental shortcuts) saturate our lives. Many
of these biases are "unconscious," and often when they are
conscious, they are supported by nothing more than a "gut
feeling." Over the years, researchers have identified an A to Z
list of biases not only based on age, gender, and race, but also
in seemingly less socially charged patterns of thinking. For
example, there is "selection bias," where one has the tendency
to notice something more when something causes one to be
more aware of it. This can be something as benign as seeing

---

[3]Simon Kuper, *Football Against the Enemy* (London: Orion, 1994),114.

more of a certain make and model of car on the road for the mere reason that one has just bought that same make and model of car. There is not necessarily a higher number of such cars on the road, but now one "sees" them more.

Biases can change. But the first step has to be recognition that they exist in the first place. A 2012 experiment on race and football "challenges" (defined as two players vying for the ball, sometimes resulting in a foul) suggested that players, fans, and referees "were faster to consider challenges made by Black players as fouls . . . [and to see] fouls made by White players as more severe."[4] More recently, professional footballers Raheem Sterling and Romelu Lukaku have spoken out how commentators often prejudice Black footballers' play as well as their off-pitch behavior. Sterling pointed out how the *Daily Mail* published an article highlighting a young Black pro as spending his salary recklessly on a new expensive mansion, but then ran another article about a young White pro as doing something worthy with his salary; both players on are the same team and both bought £2 million homes for their mothers.[5] Belgian international Lukaku also has discussed at length the portrayal of Black players, noting how broadcasters often talk about his strength, size, and pace,

[4]Wagner-Egger, P., Gygax, P., & Ribordy, F., "Racism in Soccer? Perception of Challenges of Black and White Players by White Referees, Soccer Players, and Fans," *Perceptual & Motor Skills*, 114 (2012), 275-289.
[5]@sterling7 *Instagram*, December 9, 2018. https://www.instagram.com/p/BrKYvF3gH9e/

but rarely if ever about his football intelligence or vision. Theirs is not anecdotal evidence. In 2021, a revelatory study of more than 2,000 remarks by broadcast commentators in the 2019-20 season in Europe's top four leagues showed how commentators tended to "praise players with lighter skin tone as more intelligent" and "players with darker skin tone as significantly more likely to be reduced to their physical characteristics or athletic abilities."[6] If broadcasters perpetuate biases, is it any wonder that fans mimic those patterns even if they aren't "conscious" of it? What would it take to subvert such patterns of thinking, to truly make the future stronger in color?

---

[6]Danny McLoughlin, "Racial Bias in Football Commentary (Study): The Pace and Power Effect." March 2, 2021. https://runrepeat.com/racial-bias-study-soccer

18 RESET

When the Bundesliga restarted in May 2020, after the first pandemic lockdown, each match began with a moment of silence for the victims of COVID-19. Players of both teams stood on the circumference of the center circle in observance. It was odd: the minute of "silence" was accompanied by some kind of piped-in, stringed instrument, classical composition. When Spain's La Liga restarted a few weeks later, the moment of silence was actually silent. The following week the Premier League observed a silent moment of silence—but with an addition. After the players stepped off the circle and headed to their positions for kick-off, there was a second moment of silence in which everyone—players, coaches, and even the referee—took a knee in support of Black Lives Matter. It was a stark contrast to the iconic image of the NFL only a few years earlier: Colin Kaepernick on his knee, followed by a very small handful of other players . . . and soon thereafter Kaepernick was out of a job indefinitely.

To an extent, the pandemic reset football. As fans were prohibited from attending live matches, players and coaches were able to take back a degree of control from a certain segment of those very fans. What do I mean? In February 2020, weeks before the worldwide shut-down of sports and almost all else, there was an emblematic racist event in the Portuguese top flight. After Porto's striker Moussa Marega scored a goal against Vitória SC, a club he played for on loan in 2016-17, he pointed to his skin in reply to racist jeers he'd received in pre-game warm-up and during the game. Some Vitória fans shouted more abuse after his action. Then some threw stadium seats at him. He gave them the double middle-finger and departed the pitch and the game, despite his teammates and coach's attempts to convince him to carry on.[1] Vitória's coach condemned the fans' behavior, as did the Prime Minister and President of Portugal. Condemnations are important, but they don't necessarily lead to immediate change. The racist actions against Marega were hardly the first or worst in the history of the game. But the pandemic kept the fans—good, bad, racist—out of the stadium. Not only did the players coordinate that knee-taking in the Premier League, but more strikingly all the players wore jerseys with "Black Lives Matter" printed in prominent letters on the back where normally their names would be. It wasn't a panacea. But it was a statement of unity. And no fan was there to

---

[1]"Porto's Moussa Marega gives Vitoria fans finger after apparent racist abuse," February 17, 2020. https://www.theguardian.com/football/2020/feb/16/porto-striker-moussa-marega-walks-off-the-pitch-racist-abuse

throw expletives or lighters or cans of beer or chairs or rocks or bags of urine.

Racism goes far beyond high-profile incidents; it permeates our thinking and our institutions. A few examples to illustrate: Only six of the 92 managers in England's top four divisions are not White men, even though about 25% of the players are people of color;[2] and, in the MLS eight out of the 26 coaches are Latinx, vastly disproportionate to the percentage (68%) of Latinx soccer viewers in the US.[3] In refereeing the story is the same; Uriah Rennie is the Premier League's latest Black referee (he retired twelve years ago), and there's never been a Black referee in the Champions League.[4]

Sports journalism is no less implicated in the discrepancy between the number of players of color and the White people (mostly men) who get to frame the narratives about them. Calum Jacobs, co-founder of *CARICOM*, a magazine dedicated to the Black experience in European football, has co-created a 15-minute documentary of poignant interviews

---

[2]Rick Kelsey, "Black football coaches: What holds us back," June 11, 2020. https://www.bbc.com/news/newsbeat-52979173

[3]"When it Comes to the Language of Fútbol, Hispanic Americans Know it Best." June 14, 2018. https://www.nielsen.com/us/en/insights/article/2018/when-it-comes-to-the-language-of-futbol-hispanic-americans-know-it-best

[4]Jack Rathborn, "Uriah Rennie demands 'words are met by action' to increase diversity among Premier League officials," *The Independent*, June 11, 2020. https://www.independent.co.uk/sport/football/premier-league/uriah-rennie-referee-black-premier-league-bame-a9560121.html

titled "Beat the Bias" in which recent Black footballers echo the racism and exploitation that Europe's first Black footballers endured for decades.[5] Like Campbell looking at the mural, Jacobs and other journalists rarely see anyone of color covering sports, and they discuss the dilemma of entering White spaces where they have to represent themselves as well as entire Black, muslim, or other non-White communities. One statistic is representative of the problem: there are no Black sports columnists (save current or ex-pro players) in any of the mainstream newspapers in the UK.[6] In addition to getting people of color into power positions in front of the camera, the aim of a new generation of activists is ontological: "To get to a space where you can go for it and not worry about what people who don't look like you are thinking."[7]

Rory Smith intimates that the concept of winning, amid other factors such as lawless social media, may be an important factor in continued systemic racism and sexism in football:

---

[5]"Beat the Bias: The Pioneers Revolutionising Football Media," accessed December 17, 2020, https://www.youtube.com/watch?v=pXUlqY4H kqQ. For a person-by-person history of the first male Black footballers in England, seek out *Football's Black Pioneers; The Stories of the First Black Players to Represent the 92 League Clubs*, by Bill Hern and David Gleave.

[6]More statistics available at The Black Collective of Media in Sport (BCOMS): https://www.bcoms.co.

[7]Jeanette Kwakye, a board member of BCOMS.

But to give it all [efforts against discrimination] the best chance of working, the sport must also seek to lower its own internal temperature a little, to be conscious of the roads it allows itself to be drawn down, to ask if it is necessary to treat defeat as disaster, if it could do a little more to inculcate a healthier environment, if it must continue to accept abuse as the dark consequence of passion.[8]

And where does the notion of "defeat as disaster" come from?

"The elephant in the room is always capitalism," the activist and scholar Angela Davis says. "Even when we fail to have an explicit conversation about capitalism, it is the driving force of so much when we talk about racism."[9] She doesn't mean only the African-American experience and the ongoing legacy of slavery. She's talking about the genocide of peoples and communities who lived in what we now call the United States. There were winners and losers, and patterns of capitalism allowed the winners to win more. Consider the big data: the disproportionate numbers and percentages of

---

[8]Rory Smith, "Soccer Isn't Blameless in Its Culture of Abuse," *The New York Times*, February 13, 2012. https://www.nytimes.com/2021/02/12/soccer/racial-abuse-britain.html

[9]Nelson George. "Angela Davis," *New York Times Magazine*, October 19, 2020. https://www.nytimes.com/interactive/2020/10/19/t-magazine/angela-davis.html

incarcerated Black men in the US; the economies of scale that not only allow but promote very small groups of White men and their companies—Facebook, Apple, Twitter, Google—to control so much of the economic as well as the social and political patterns of the world. Professional football may be at the top of the capitalist tower: to win is to make money and to make money is to win. Which almost sounds like Keats' mellifluous, if dubious, epigram, "beauty is truth and truth is beauty."

How does one begin to deal with the through lines of "win at all costs" and "defeat as disaster" and "us versus them," which after all is what fandom is largely based on? By changing the discourse. The moment, for example, that Twitter finally suspended President Trump's account, much of our discourse transformed literally overnight. When I say discourse, I mean language—the power and dissemination of words and thus thinking. When I say dissemination, I mean spread—like a virus. The analogue cannot be overemphasized.

19 THE BEST SEATS

Whenever I asked my father if we could go see the Chicago Cubs baseball team play at Wrigley Field, he always had the same reply: "Why drive all the way into the city when the best seats are here at home?" Of course I would argue about *the experience* of sitting behind the famous ivy wall in the bleachers amid rapturous fans, but he would wave it off kindly, saying it was too expensive. I thought he was being overly parsimonious, a word I learned alongside "asinine" and "facetious" in our family's pet phrases.

On the 20th anniversary of the publication of *Fever Pitch*, Nick Hornby's memoir of his obsessed fandom of Arsenal, he lamented that in the 1970s it cost only 15 pence to see his favorite club—as a kid he could afford to go to matches all the time.[1] Today kids can't do that because the ticket cost is prohibitive; accordingly, the age of fans

---

[1]Jamie Doward, "Fever Pitch author Nick Hornby says beautiful game has lost its way," *The Guardian*, March 3, 2012. https://www.theguardian.com/books/2012/mar/04/nick-hornby-fever-pitch-anniversary

in stadiums has risen. In 1968, the average age of a fan in the West End of Manchester United's Old Trafford was 17; in 2008, it was over 40.[2] High ticket prices run through pretty much all elite sports. In January 2020, for instance, I took my eldest son to see our first New Orleans Pelicans basketball game in the Smoothie King Center. Actually it wasn't really to see all of the Pelicans—it was to see the rookie phenom Zion Williamson who was finally back from a half-season-long injury. It cost $175 for two decent tickets (a Hanukkah/Christmas present I'd given us), and once inside we spent another $40 on hotdogs, peanuts, and a beer. I have to say that what I ultimately remember about the game was what happened before it even began: the moving tribute to Kobe Bryant who had died that morning in a helicopter crash.[3]

If today you can't afford to see pro athletes live with any regularity, two aspects of watching at home have improved dramatically. First, you can now view matches in high definition, where 30-plus cameras are in operation, which means you can see the stitching on the ball at kick-off, the blades of shorn grass on a player's chin or forehead after

---

[2]Adrian Tempany, *And the Sun Shines Now: How Hillsborough and the Premier League Changed Britain* (London: Faber & Faber, 2016), 162.
[3]That evening when I watched two La Liga fixtures, there was a long moment of silence before the matches in honor of Bryant. He was an avid soccer fan, having grown up partly in Italy, and he credited much of his vision on the court to his playing soccer.

going to ground—not to mention the variety of camera shots and angles played any number of times after a fine shot or feint or pass or dribble or atrocious foul. Second, you can watch games from all across the globe. Following Europe's top flights has been easy for some time, but now you can watch top leagues or tournaments in Mexico, India, China, and Africa. This seems obvious to point out in our growth-obsessed digital environment, but as commentator Paul Kennedy reminded us after Maradona's death in 2020, it used to be all but impossible to see any matches in the US, even those with the world's top players:

Maradona . . . was rarely seen on American television. If you were lucky, you lived in a major city with an ethnic television channel and saw a couple of minutes of Napoli highlights each week . . . [Italy's] Serie A in the 1980s was the league, with perhaps the greatest collection of talent ever assembled in one place. Maradona at Napoli. Michel Platini and Zbigniew Boniek at Juventus. Ruud Gullit, Frank Rijkaard and Marco van Basten at AC Milan. Lothar Matthaeus, Andreas Brehme and Jürgen Klinsmann. Plus all the Azzurri from Italy's 1982 World Cup championship team. But there was no way to follow them.[4]

---

[4]Paul Kennedy, "Diego, we hardly knew ye," November 27, 2020. https://www.socceramerica.com/publications/article/87394/diego-we-hardly-knew-ye.html

Not only can you follow them, but you can record them and watch matches whenever you like . . . except when you can't. Women's football is still difficult to keep up with because of the meager quantity of broadcasts, even when it comes to big stars like US national Alex Morgan or Danish national Nadia Nadim.[5]

Before live football broadcasts returned during the pandemic, I went back and watched all the Bundesliga games I'd missed the previous season. (Maybe my father was right after all: the best seats are in the family room on the couch.) When the pre-recorded matches ran out, I began watching matches that had just restarted in the States. The National Women's Soccer League (NWSL) came back a few weeks before the MLS. At the first match between North Carolina and Portland, part of the women's Challenge Cup, the players wore Black Lives Matter shirts and kneeled in a moment of silence. I couldn't help but feel that the US was late to the party. And yet being late doesn't necessarily mean it's less significant. Some weeks later, in the last match of the regular season of the USL Championship (second division in the US men's system), San Diego Loyal SC actually left the field in protest. A player from the opposing team, Phoenix

---

[5]For her skill and vision, Nadim is wonderful to watch as a footballer, but her story is perhaps more wonderful: a refugee who escaped Taliban-controlled Afghanistan, who speaks 11 languages, and who is completing medical school to be a reconstructive surgeon.

Rising's Junior Flemmings, had hurled the slur "bati boy," a Jamaican epithet which is something like "butt boy," at Colin Martin, an openly gay Loyal player. This in a league where not many are openly gay.[6]

When Martin first tried to tell the referee about the slur, the referee thought Martin was calling him gay and pulled out the red card. The matter was taken to the sideline, where the referee admitted to Rising's coach, Rick Schantz, and Loyal's coach, Landon Donovan, that he didn't hear the slur and/or didn't know what it meant. Schantz refused to pull his player from the match, saying to Donovan: "They're competing. How long have you been playing soccer?" The implication being that abusive trash talk happens all the time on the pitch.

All of this occurred a week after another Loyal player was the object of a racial slur in another match. As Schantz and Donovan continued to discuss, you could see Loyal's new motto in the background on the big screen inside the stadium: *I will speak, I will act. Black Lives Matter.* The incident happened at the end of the first half. As soon as the ball was kicked-off for the second half, Loyal players turned and walked off the pitch. I have never witnessed anything

---

[6]Homophobic slurs may not be as prevalent, or as reported on, as racist ones in football, but they are no less malicious. Certain fans of Mexico's national team have a specific anti-gay chant (*Puto!*) for opposing goalkeepers; the chant is so loud you can hear it via broadcast.

like it. Loyal was winning the match (3-1) and their forfeiture meant they would not go to the playoffs. As the team walked off in unison, you could see Colin Martin pulling his jersey up to his face in pain. Later, Donovan said in an interview: "They were very clear in that moment . . . even though they were beating one of the best teams in the league handedly. But they said that doesn't matter, there are things more important in life and we have to stick up for what we believe in."[7]

This is not symbolism; it is admirable, real action. Someone commented on Twitter, however, that there was likely a time when Donovan himself growing up playing the game, or even as a pro at some point, used homophobic slurs or other kinds of slurs against a foreign player. I remember very well, for instance, that it used to be the norm to use the term "gay" as a slur of many kinds in the 1980s and early 90s. The point is not that Donovan is a hypocrite (and he may never have used homophobic language). Instead, I see the point to be that the patterns of a society can change, and language is at the center of that change. How we talk about the game of football matters to how we think about it, play it, and watch it.

One more aspect seems important to what happened in the Loyal-Rising match: the stadium was empty of fans.

---

[7] "USL's San Diego Loyal forfeit in protest, alleging anti-gay slur." October 1, 2020. https://www.espn.com/sports/soccer/story/_/id/30013159/usl-san-diego-loyal-forfeit-protest-alleging-anti-gay-slur

Would they have made a difference in the players' decision to abandon the game? It's hard to tell. But the fact that fans were not present raises again a question that may take years to answer with any clarity: How might the absence of live fans improve the game?

20 HACKING, DIVING, HUGGING

I first started watching football broadcasts in a serious way during the 2018 World Cup. Along with half the planet's population who apparently viewed at least some portion of the month-long competition, I enjoyed the high quality play and the final between Croatia and France, including following the very likeable Croatian midfielder and playmaker Luka Modrić. But many times I couldn't believe what I was seeing. The referees called fouls for what looked to me like simply hard tackles. I'd yelp at the TV: *Yellow card? But he got the ball!* As a kid playing in the 1970s and 80s, as long as you got the slightest of touches on the ball, there was no foul—no matter how hard the opposing player went down. And they went down hard often. From ten years old and on, I played fullback usually on the left side because being cross-dominant I was the closest our team had to a left-footed player. Slide-tackles were my specialty.

When I played in college in the late 80s and early 90s, the game was even rougher. Straight away from kick-off, strikers and fullbacks would trash talk and grunt at each other while physically battling over who was quicker, tougher, and better positioned. There was no zone-marking; it was all man-to-man. Today, this kind of "hard" play is mentioned occasionally in a quasi-nostalgic way. When Diego Maradona died at age 60, however, discussion about "old school" hacking resurfaced. Mostly penned years before he died, Maradona's obituaries focused on his 1986 World Cup "Hand of God" goal and "Goal of the Century," and his notorious drug use and outlandish behavior. In subsequent days, though, commentators began a more interesting thread, exemplified by Barney Ronay's writing:

> Maradona emerged as football was beginning the journey towards the current germ-free environment, a place where every surface is sealed, every space safe, every variable controlled. The most obvious change is the level of physical danger. To embark on a dribble, to attempt to assert your skill, was an act of calculated self-destruction. Basically, Maradona had the crap kicked out of him. He was fouled constantly and brutally.[1]

Ronay goes on to detail how the epitome of the brutality came when Andoni Goikoetxea, nicknamed "The Butcher of Bilbao," purposely broke Maradona's ankle: "with a sound like a piece of wood splitting . . . the world's most expensive

---

[1]"Brave, intelligent Diego Maradona was a man who moved through different air," *The Guardian*, November 27, 2020. https://www.theguardian.com/football/2020/nov/27/brave-intelligent-diego-maradona-was-a-man-who-moved-through-different-air

footballer was carried off on a blanket, then driven to hospital in a small, borrowed van."

Although I don't think many lament that intentional brutality is no longer part of today's professional game, there has been one particular consequence: the dive. Or the flop. Or the "simulation," as in feigning a real fall, a real foul. If you ask an evolutionary biologist, running is simply "controlled falling." The gluteus maximus muscle clenches when we run, preventing our bodies from pitching too far forward and tumbling over. So if you're a striker, you let your gluteus maximus go when you want to fall accidentally on purpose. To my nine-year-old daughter watching the famed Neymar lay on the ground writhing, such dives look like something else: "Why do the players always do somersaults when they get fouled?"

Neymar got the call that time. To put it more clearly: the referee gave it to him. It was a subjective judgement and, like the majority of calls, no matter how hard a referee tries to be "objective," adhering to FIFA's rulebook, it's almost impossible. Referees at the pro level make 245 decisions per game on average—almost three per minute—giving them plenty of chances to screw things up.[2] Moreover, the rulebook is not always crystal clear in the first place. The official handball rule, for example, has changed so many times in the modern game that there's almost always a debate over each potential

[2]Stuart Carrington, *Blowing the Whistle: The Psychology of Football Refereeing* (UK: Dark River, 2019), 18.

instance of it, especially with respect to whether or not the arm in question was in a "natural" position when the ball struck it. Such a judgement call is rarely helped even with video review.

At a certain level, subjectivity is simply part of the game's variability. One referee will allow more physicality between players, while another will call anything that even resembles a jostling. And while goal line technology (a camera) can show us whether or not a ball is definitively all the way over the goal line, technology can't show us with any definition whether the defender in the case above actually clipped Neymar on the calf, or Neymar threw himself to ground chiefly of his own accord. As many commentators regularly point out, slow-motion video replay distorts the nature of a potential foul: slow motion often makes the foul look harsher than it was.

Certain fans believe that the dive issue is really a matter of ethics. The argument goes that simulation isn't "honest" behavior and displays "a willingness to cheat," and when a dive leads to, say, a game-changing penalty kick, the game itself gets corrupted.[3] Others argue that diving is part and parcel of the modern game and players are cleverly acting within the rules. As well, if a player gets "caught" faking an action, they are punished accordingly with a yellow card. To me, there is something else: a footballer who flops regularly is not a very

---

[3] Alejandro Chacoff, "The fall: how diving became football's worst crime," *The Guardian*, April 6, 2016. https://www.theguardian.com/football/2016/apr/06/the-fall-how-diving-became-football-worst-crime

impressive model to work from; a young player would be better off spending her time learning more practical skills.

In the history of contemporary dives, the one I recall most is Jürgen Klinsmann's epic act in the 1990 World Cup match between Argentina and West Germany. While being clipped, Klinsmann not only flies up into the air but on landing bounces around as though in seizure. Even though the player who fouled Klinsmann earned a red card, observers chastised his melodramatic feat. Four years later, when Klinsmann made the move to Tottenham, he revived the dive—but with a variation. After scoring his first goal as a Hotspur, he and his teammates took coordinated dives together, a pre-planned act that led to others, including kids, emulating the celebration dive and slide we see so often today. I have to say that I've never really understood the wild celebration after scoring a goal—a goal that may have involved as much chance as skill. In pickup games, there is often a yelp and a few high-fives or fist-bumps . . . but a dive-slide? It'd be uncouth. There are some professionals who don't seem to go in for all the exaggerated enthusiasm. There is the occasion, as well, when a player who left a club amicably, a club she played on for years, then plays against that very club. If she scores, she purposefully doesn't celebrate; her countenance that of someone just doing her job, like delivering the mail.

When I do see a celebration of footballers huddled together or smashed up against one another, I'm struck by the bodies embracing or lips kissing each other's cheeks or heads—a sight I witness almost never anywhere else. I'm struck, too, that I have a different feeling when the bodies are all men's as compared to all women's. The iconoclastic artist Barbara Kruger addresses just this notion in a 1981 collage artwork that features a photo of a small group of men in suits horsing around at some kind of formal event.[4]

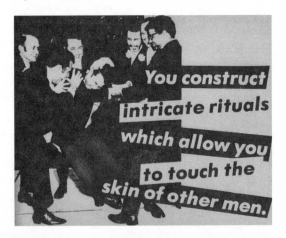

About the work, Kruger says:

It has to do with the notion of a comfort or discomfort with sameness and difference and that sports, for instance, is a way that men can be allowed to have physical contact that is disallowed in a homophobic culture—not only

---

[4]Barbara Kruger. *Untitled (You construct intricate rituals which allow you to touch the skin of other men)*, 1981. Courtesy of the artist and Sprüth Magers.

in the playing of the game but also in the viewing of the game. Sports promote a kind of romance or a group understanding and intimacy about the notion of teams, about men being together and men's bodies being together.[5]

While Kruger's insight might apply to any sport or activity where men's bodies are in close contact, football may just be our best example as it's played and watched all over the world by millions of boys and men.[6]

---

[5]"Resisting Reductivism & Breaking the Bubble." Interview with Barbara Kruger. https://art21.org/read/barbara-kruger-resisting-reductivism-breaking-the-bubble/

[6]Goal celebration in Leicester City's 1-0 win over AFC Bournemouth on February 1, 2014. Courtesy of Simon Kimber.

As far as how this plays out locally, I can speak only from my experience. There were no hugs, group or otherwise, when I was a kid playing 40 years ago or on my US college team. But in the last 10 years pre-pandemic, our pickup games included numerous one-on-one man-hugs before, during, and after the game. At the moment, there are only waves or fist-bumps . . . except for a few of us who sometimes can't help ourselves; we embrace each other while holding our breath.

21 INTERSECTIONALITY

Although she is two years younger than me, my sister played soccer often better than I did when we were kids in the 1980s. She had a beautiful touch and strong foot, and could beat me one-on-one in the backyard. Always a stellar athlete, she was the star of her soccer and softball teams, and never bragged, not even humbly. From an early age, I knew that girls could play sports as well or better than boys. Yet I am guilty of not telling my sister how proud I was of her back then. There is a great difference between tolerance and appreciation.

In the first chapter of *Fever Pitch*, Hornby mentions girls briefly: "Maybe a nine-year-old girl in the nineties would feel that she had just as much right to go to a game as we did. But in 1969 in our town, this was not an idea that had much currency, and my sister had to stay at home with her mum and play with dolls."[1]

Hornby's book was first published in 1992.

---

[1] *Fever Pitch*, 10. Hornby's book was written, it would seem, partially in response to Bill Buford's *Among the Thugs*, published two years earlier. Hornby writes in the last paragraph of the introduction: "and I have read books written, for

In 1999, the US soccer star Brandi Chastain pulled off her jersey after scoring the game-winning penalty kick to beat China in the Women's World Cup. Her black sports bra was revealed for all the world to see: 90,125 fans at the Rose Bowl and 40 million TV viewers.

In between *Fever Pitch* and Chastain's bra, the term "soccer mom" spawned. It was in the summer of 1996 and the lead-up to the US Presidential election between incumbent Bill Clinton and Senator Bob Dole. "Soccer mom" became the notation for a group of swing voters that the parties and the media targeted as crucial to winning the election. Although women did in the end provide the swing vote for Clinton (54% of women and 43% of men voted for Clinton), as political scientist Susan J. Carroll writes:

> The focus on the soccer mom allowed both the media and the campaigns to appear to be responsive to the concerns of women voters while actually ignoring the vast majority of women . . . Clinton was reelected to office without campaigning aggressively on (or, in some cases, even seriously addressing) a variety of issues central to both feminists and to women who are not white, middle-class, suburban mothers of young children.[2]

---

want of a better word, by hooligans, but at least 95 percent of the millions who watch games every year have never hit anyone in their lives."
[2] Susan J. Carroll, "The Disempowerment of the Gender Gap: Soccer Moms and the 1996 Elections," *PS: Political Science and Politics*, Vol. 32, No. 1, 1999, 11.

That last bit—White, middle-class, suburban mothers—is usually what soccer mom refers to, though the mental image may include a minivan or now an SUV. Even with Title IX, the 1972 anti-discrimination and civil rights law that has helped bring some equity to US higher education, the disparity today between women's and men's sports is still vast.[3] The money is unequal, the coverage is unequal, and we still often call football that women play "women's football." The September 2020 edition of *World Soccer* was devoted to "the 500 most important players on the planet"; apparently only 14 are women. In fact, this issue marked the first time women have been included in the 500. According to the assistant editor's note, "[the list] is not definitive, nor is it about who is the best, but rather a guide to the players we think you should know about in the upcoming season."

What happens when you're not allowed to play or even to watch football? Prohibited not because of expense but

---

[3]Historian Barbara Winslow describes what life was like for young women before Title IX: "Young women were not admitted into many colleges and universities, athletic scholarships for women were rare, and math and science was a realm reserved for boys. Girls square danced instead of playing sports, studied home economics instead of training for "male-oriented" (read: higher-paying) trades. Girls could become teachers and nurses, but not doctors or principals; women rarely were awarded tenure and even more rarely appointed college presidents. There was no such thing as sexual harassment because 'boys will be boys, after all, and if a student got pregnant, her formal education ended. Graduate professional schools openly discriminated against women."

because of cultural barriers. In some Islamic countries, most notably in Iran, laws and authorities (i.e. men) forbid women from playing, attending, or watching broadcast matches. In *Pelada*, Gwen Oxenham finds young women in Tehran who break the law to play in games of 2 or 3-a-side. The match may last for only 15 minutes, but you can still hear and see the joy on their faces, the same joy that boys and men experience. In fact, historians tell us that women have played football or its precursors since antiquity in various societies. In the Later Han dynasty in China, for instance, first-century frescoes depict female figures playing the ancient ball game of *tsu chu*.[4]

When the rules of modern football were set down in England in 1863, women organized matches as men did. In 1921, however, the English Football Association formally banned women from the game. The problem? Men in charge felt threatened. Women's matches were drawing tens of thousands of fans to stadiums—more fans than those at many of the men's games. The ban in England continued until the late 1960s. Other countries also banned women from the game, including Brazil from 1941 to 1979, citing that "violent" sports are "not suitable for the female body"; Germany from 1955 to 1970, with statements like "In the

---

[4] *The Global Game, A Football Monthly.* Vol 1, No. 7, August 2003. https://web.archive.org/web/20060522002448/http://www.theglobalgame.com/pdf/07_ebook.pdf

fight for the ball, the feminine grace vanishes, body and soul will inevitably suffer harm"; and Spain from 1935 to 1970, where the president of the football federation said, "I am not against women's football, but I do not like it either. From the aesthetic point of view, a woman in a t-shirt and pants is not preferable. Any regional dress would suit her better."[5]

I try to take in these statements after watching a number of YouTube videos of girls playing football in Jordan. In one, a girl of about seven tells us: "Soccer relaxes me. I feel good when I play. And so I start to play all the time." A girl of about eleven adds, "I want to deliver a message to the world. That we refugees have dreams that can be realized through football. This game gives up hope." YouTube leads me to other videos and other barriers. In a TED Talk from 2014, Honey Thaljieh, the pride of football in Palestine, talks about how her identity—female, Palestinian, Christian, Arab, impoverished, and disabled through injury—prevented her playing football but also allowed her to make a difference in taking down some barriers. Football, in other words, was the vehicle for change.[6] In Afghanistan, 20-year-old Sabria Nawrozi, who captains the Afghan team Herat Storm, argues

---

[5]James Dator, "A short history of the banning of women's soccer," July 6, 2019. https://www.sbnation.com/soccer/2019/7/6/18658729/banning-womens-soccer-world-cup-effects
[6]TEDxZurich, "Honey, football changed my life," November 20, 2014. https://www.youtube.com/watch?v=SOB7UwEeo0w

that Islam is not incompatible with what she loves: "What are they [the Taliban] going to do? Say that we can only play in a burka? . . . I wear an Islamic hijab and I play football. It's a pleasure for us to play this way, because it shows everybody that we are Muslims. That's a source of pride for us."[7]

Some prohibitive rules and patterns may be changing, if ever so slowly. In January 2018, Saudi Arabia allowed women to legally enter stadiums to watch matches. Six months later women were allowed to get a driver's license. And in February 2020, after years of women forming their own recreational leagues, Saudis formally established a women's football league across the country. In Qatar, more women than men go to university, and women have been officially allowed to play football since 2009. But the notion and practice of women playing still runs against tradition; Qatar has a women's national team but it's made up almost entirely of expat Qataris. Although the country will host World Cup 2022, a possible catalyst for women playing football, the tournament has already been overshadowed by two problems: corruption that led to Qatar being awarded the World Cup in 2010; and, continued human rights abuses of thousands of migrant workers who are building stadiums

---

[7]"Women Of Afghanistan Won't Give Up Their Soccer Dreams." November 8, 2020. https://www.npr.org/sections/goatsandsoda/2020/11/08/9320688 05/women-of-afghanistan-wont-give-up-their-soccer-dreams

and infrastructure for the tournament. A conversative tally of deaths of these workers, who come from the poorest areas of India, Bangladesh, Nepal, Sri Lanka, Kenya, Philippines, and elsewhere, is around 6,500.[8]

If there are women in head coverings trying to play the game they love on one side of the world, there are women's bodies being displayed as empowerment on the other. In 2019, four US soccer players—Alex Morgan, Crystal Dunn, Abby Dahlkemper, and Megan Rapinoe—appeared in the *Sports Illustrated* Swimsuit Issue.[9] Along with being named Sportsperson of the Year for 2019, Rapinoe also is the first openly gay women to be featured in the issue. Like Thaljieh in Palestine, Rapinoe has parlayed her football notoriety into social justice. A few days after Colin Kaepernick took a knee during the US national anthem in 2016, Megan Rapinoe did the same. She was the first bigtime player outside of the NFL to support his protest, and she was roundly rebuked.[10] Four years later, when the Black Lives Matter movement restarted in early summer 2020 and players in European football began

[8]"Revealed: 6,500 migrant workers have died in Qatar as it gears up for World Cup," *The Guardian*, February 23, 2021. https://www.theguardian.c om/global-development/2021/feb/23/revealed-migrant-worker-deaths-qa tar-fifa-world-cup-2022

[9]*Sports Illustrated,* May 8, 2019. https://swimsuit.si.com/news/uswnt-gende r-equality-si-swimsuit-2019

[10]Euan McKirdy, "Megan Rapinoe takes knee in solidarity with Kaepernick," CNN. September 5, 2016. https://edition.cnn.com/2016/09/05/sport/megan -rapinoe-colin-kaepernick-anthem-kneel

taking a knee, the newly elected US Soccer Federation president personally apologized to Rapinoe. The same week, Rapinoe appeared on *The Late Show with Stephen Colbert,* restating what she has many times: "This country very much glorifies its athletes and gives us these huge platforms. So, I'm going to leverage the platform for what I think is good." She continued, "We can't say 'All Lives Matter' anymore because the All Lives' house isn't on fire, it's just the Black Lives right now."

Rapinoe's efforts are examples of different movements working toward mutually beneficial goals. First used by scholar Kimberlé Crenshaw in 1989, intersectionality is the term for what has taken root in recent years: the concept identifies the concentricity among disadvantaged or oppressed people based on gender, race, class, religion, or any combination. So when Rapinoe writes in the introduction to her 2020 memoir *One Life* about taking a knee in solidarity with Kaepernick, it was in part because she knew a similar kind of oppression: "I wasn't just familiar with the politics behind Colin's protest; I felt them, in my own way. I know what it means to look at the flag and not have it protect all of your liberties."

Rapinoe is not an uncomplicated person; she was raised in a conservative Christian town, voted for George W. Bush in 2004, and has an older brother who used to be a heroin addict and white supremacist gang member. If I needed any evidence that Rapinoe's message is as much about social justice as it is about football, it was right in front of me the day I pre-ordered her memoir. Scrolling down the Amazon page, the nifty "frequently bought together" feature included Rapinoe's along with Ruth Bader Ginsburg's and Barack Obama's memoirs. Indeed, the most important aspect of Rapinoe's book is the intersectionality vein; her bottom line is that football is a platform for social change, an idea that is being leveraged by many footballers now. At the same time Rapinoe's book was released in October 2020, Manchester United's Marcus Rashford had collected a million signatures on a petition to get the British government to provide free meals to kids at school. Rashford's initial work toward feeding children began during the UK lockdown that spring. Quickly his philanthropy turned to activism. An activist at age 23, he's declared "to fight for the rest of his life" to end hunger for children throughout the UK. In case you didn't already know, Rashford is Black.

22 LIVE FOOTBALL IN A PANDEMIC

This is the thing about taking antidepressants: they don't allow tears. At least not mine, with which tears can be conjured up only after a certain number of drinks and an appropriate traumatic event. Fortunately, my digestive system usually prohibits anything more than three alcoholic beverages before it revolts; for that reason, and perhaps that reason alone, I shall never be an alcoholic.

And yet there I was throughout most of 2020 cracking the first beer after the first coffee, trying to figure out the best way to reach a brain chemistry that would allow me not to lose my patience with one of my children. Alcohol as lubricant rather than intoxicant. My wife and I were now either Zooming continually with colleagues or students, or helping one of our three kids with their online school, which meant figuring out how to be an eighth grade teacher, a fifth grader teacher, and a pre-K teacher. The four-year-old was increasingly the most difficult. When our neighbor asked him how online school was going, he spat back: "All I do is sit sit sit sit sit sit sit sit!" Usually he sat on my lap, though at times he'd sit under the desk and I'd have to try to angle the video camera toward him. Six weeks into the fall school year, I needed a break from the household, and I knew my wife needed a break from me: playing three pickup games a week was doing wonders for my mental health, but it was perhaps undoing hers.

At the end of September 2020, my ten-year-old daughter and I took a road trip to Frisco, Texas, to attend a live match between FC Dallas and Orlando City. Major League Soccer had already held an "MLS is Back" tournament in July, but FC Dallas had not taken part because 12 players and one coach had tested positive for COVID-19. This match was one of the first to which MLS would allow fans to return at 25% capacity, about 5,000 of us.

FC Dallas' Toyota Stadium also houses the US Soccer Hall of Fame, so the day before the match we decided to visit. It's predictably small; Samara and I traversed the space in about 20 minutes. There were a couple of "interactive" virtual stations, one in which you juggle a ball. Samara juggled 41 times, which is curious because in that thing called "real life" she can't juggle past two. I suppose the point isn't about juggling; it's getting kids interested in the game. The second virtual station allowed her to take penalty kicks. She enjoyed this one a little more. But all I could focus on were the goalposts: they were square, not rounded as has been mandated since 1987. I thought: Why can't we get the details right in the US? Samara did appreciate the four World Cup trophies the Women's National Team has garnered over the years. "The rest, Dad," she said, "was kinda lame." We bought her big brother a US Men's National Team jersey—blue with stylized camouflage—and a pack of Premier League trading cards for her little brother, not only because I knew he wouldn't know even the biggest stars from the MLS pack, but also because Premier League cards were free if I used my Chase Bank Visa. "Now that's America," I said to the clerk who feigned a smile.

As we drove back to the hotel, through the suburban hellscape of concrete, strip malls, tangle of overpasses, underpasses, and highways, I had that old, distinct, and urgent desire to blow my brains out—to pull into the parking lot of Academy Sports, walk in and purchase a handgun in 15 minutes, and complete the job in the car. Was it the pandemic—the morning's news had told me that now 202,000 souls were lost to the virus—or was it simply the waxing of my depression? Either way, the traffic on the roads and the shoppers and the eaters in restaurants and the people in parking lots without masks exacerbated my ill-feeling. Harsh white sunlight began blasting off vehicles' chrome and into my eyes; I was on the verge of having a panic attack at 65 mph. Samara could tell that something was off. I exited and pulled into an auto dealership, some kind of immaculate, high-end, Audi-BMW-Mercedes-Lexus place.

"Daddy, where are we going?" I didn't know, and I didn't want to say that I didn't know. Some people experience shortness of breath or increased heartbeat. I just feel at once flattened, as though my insides are imploding, and zoomed out as though everything is happening around me and I'm no longer part of it yet I'm still a body in motion. After a long silent moment, she said, "Can we eat? I'm hungry." I looked over and up at the building. Three flags blown hard by the wind. "Texas is a strange place," I said, "the only state allowed to fly their state flag as high as the US flag." She may have nodded. I didn't look her way. I slowly watched myself take my foot off the brake and get back on the highway. Only one exit to the hotel. Inside our room, she happily ate leftover tacos and I retreated to the safety of a Xanax and a hot shower.

The next day we hit the Museum of Illusions and the Perot Museum of Nature and Science. Samara enjoyed the exhibits, and I enjoyed the observance of social distancing. Driving back out to Toyota Stadium for the match, there was little traffic and on entering the stadium parking lot we saw fans wearing masks. I was relieved. People flowed into the east gate thoughtfully. Samara and I climbed the final stairs and spread out before us lay the beauty of the stadium, half a clam cracked open. It was her first time attending live professional soccer. She hugged me. "Thank you so much, Daddy, for taking me to Dallas and to see this game!"

We found our seats on the fifty-yard line (the stadium apparently also hosts occasional American football games). I counted eight seats between us and the next closest fans. The sun set directly in front of us, medium lovely and orange-pink. Sprinklers shot out rainbows of water across the pitch.

Samara asked, "Aren't they going to slip?" I explained how the ball will move faster making the match literally more fluid.

Then came the stirrings of a song: "The Star-Spangled Banner." I'd almost forgotten the pre-game ritual. Fans began rising from their seats and turning around to face the American flag, which was behind us, hands over their hearts. Samara had never experienced the anthem before, but she mimicked others. She stood and turned. Wanting to see what the players would do, I sat and looked to the middle of the pitch. Players from both teams formed a single line in the center, the referees separating them. From left to right, the Dallas players immediately went down on a knee, a few with fists in the air, and like dominoes the four referees took knees, as did some of the Orlando players. But then the dominoes seemed to get confused about whether to fall or half-fall or remain standing. In the end, four Orlando players took knees and seven remained standing with arms interlocked.

The anthem began.

"Daddy, stand up."

"I'm not going to."

"Daddy?!"

As much as I didn't want to embarrass her, I just couldn't get my legs to budge. Something inside me was repulsed. And then it came out: "Four hundred years of enslaving Black people—or worse. I can't stand for that . . . that *thing*."

She stood, and I sat and observed everyone else looking behind me. I pulled out my phone and snapped photos, though I didn't know why exactly. For a future history lesson?

For the book I was writing? Or just in case one of these patriots was going to get in my face and I'd need empirical evidence?

A teenager stared at me in bewilderment. I thought about telling him that his mask had slipped down.[1]

I looked around to see what the Black fans were doing: all in my view were standing, most with hands over hearts. I could be wrong, but I imagine they found it easier to go along with all the White people around them than to cause a stir by sitting or raising an arm. I am White; I had the privilege of sitting without reprisal.

---

[1] Author photo, September 2020.

The song ended. Fans turned and took their seats. The match began.

After an early solid attempt on goal by Dallas, Orlando dominated the first half—ball possession and shots on goal. At one point, while trainers attended to an injured player, I heard fake fan noise being piped in. It continued after the injury was dealt with, and could be heard as a murmur underneath the shouts of the goalkeepers directing defensive players. I pointed out the noise to Samara. "But we're real fans who can make real noise," she said. I nodded and recounted that when I watch a La Liga or Bundesliga game on TV, the default audio is fake crowd sounds and I can never figure out how to get natural sounds to be the default.

Soon we discovered that perhaps the fake fan noise was to drown out the actual fan noise, namely a lone bald, bearded heckler twenty rows in front of us. He'd yell at the referee each time a call didn't go for the home team. At first this was somewhat entertaining, but The Lone Heckler, as Samara and I began calling him, ratcheted it up louder and louder. In the second half, his commentary turned more abusive. With only five minutes left in regulation time, The Lone Heckler screamed an imprecation I couldn't quite comprehend but which prompted the stadium announcer to broadcast a message: *Derogatory language toward referees will not be tolerated and could result in suspension of fans from the game.* The message went unheeded. When the match ended abruptly in stoppage time, right as Dallas was about to cross the ball into the box, The Lone Heckler went absolutely mad, cussing out all four yellow-shirted referees as they calmly walked off the pitch and into the bowels of the stadium.

On the way to the car I didn't know what to tell my daughter—that The Lone Heckler was an anomaly? That some people are just jerks? That at least there were no brawls? Ultimately I made a bad joke about how the guy could at least have kept his mask on so that his spittle didn't shoot everywhere.

Weeks later, my mind returned to the image of that spittle. It was days after Biden beat Trump and I was trying to escape the headlines by watching my nightly match: a Chinese Super League fixture between two top teams. The British announcer didn't mention it at all, but I was shocked by what I saw in the stands: loads of fans and not one wore a mask. At halftime I looked up the COVID-19 stats: the entire country of China had 13 new cases that day. The day before there had been more cases in one wing of the White House.[2]

---

[2] As of November 14, 2020 the total deaths per 100,000 people in the US was 74; in China it was .32.

23 CHILD'S PLAY

Innocence and experience: four adults shepherding a herd of four-year-olds chasing after a ball. There is the requisite kid in the corner—the one on top of first base (this is a baseball field, not a soccer pitch) trying to crawl away. There is also the requisite kid whom the parent can't get to participate—that boy in front of the little goal, the same type of pop-up goal we use in pickup.[1] That boy, by the way, is my son Jonah, and I couldn't get him to join the others despite any number of bribes. For the ten Saturdays that made up the "season," I could get him to join the game only twice, and with me in tow. And I really tried, not because I wanted him to participate for the sake of it, but because he is quite good at the game, having played since he could walk.

For little kids, the most obvious parameter of the game is also often the hardest to follow: *No hands!* Parents often chide their kids about the rule, but I know coaches who advise parents to lighten up: if a child uses hands once in a while, it's okay; the point is to get the child interested in the game. Even if they have played for a year or two, you'll still see the occasional seven- or eight-year-old instinctively stick out a hand for the ball. As neuroscientist Jeffrey Holt explains, there is good reason for this:

> In the sporting world, the hand is a major advantage. Compare the size of the net or the difference in score between soccer and basketball. Hands do make a difference. Yet, since soccer eliminates the use of hands and focuses on the feet, soccer emphasizes another powerful human capacity: the plasticity of the human brain and

---

[1]Author photo, January 2020.

its ability to learn and be shaped by experience. The feet, the principal instruments of soccer, are represented by a very small region of cortex in the average human brain. Remarkably, this feeble cortical representation is not set in stone . . . the ability of the human brain to be remolded and learn from experience is so pervasive in humans that I would argue it is our greatest evolutionary advantage.[2]

It can seemingly take a long while for a child to use their feet with dexterity. Before long, though, they develop the patterns of touch and kick and trap—and they are incredibly good imitators and soon pick up on what they see in each other and who is around them. And who precisely is around them? Parents.

Have you ever witnessed parents scream from the sidelines *Come on, boot the ball!* or *What were you thinking!*? As a kid, I would turn to those elders and bite my tongue: *Don't you know that we already understand when we make a mistake?* As an adult, I've seen parents argue with referees to the extent of pushing and ejections from the sidelines. It happens far more than you might think. In fact, I can't think of the last time I watched a youth match when there weren't

---

[2]Jeffrey Holt, "Thinking With Your Feet: How Soccer Rewires Your Brain," *WBUR*, June 10, 2014. https://www.wbur.org/cognoscenti/2014/06/10/soccer-brain-jeffrey-holt

at least two or three parents bellowing from the sidelines at the kids or the referee. The problem is rampant in many youth sports. Hockey Canada has even parodied the issue in an effort to address the problem. In one of their promos, a kid of about ten lectures his dad who is about to putt on the golf course: "Don't slouch . . . and don't screw up! What are you doing?! Keep your eye on the ball." After his dad misses the putt, the son intones, "That was pathetic!" His dad weakly replies "Sorry," and the son says, "Yeah, well, sorry doesn't cut it!"[3]

As children grow older winning becomes more important—at least for their parents. As Adrian Tempany says about football today, "The irony is that parents are probably investing more time and interest in their children's play and leisure activities than any generation of parents before them. However, this is precisely the problem: when adults invest, they usually want a stake in the outcome."[4] The fiscal language is no accident. In the States, the system of youth soccer is one of hot competition in which "travel teams" or quasi-academy set-ups require payment. It's been dubbed "pay-to-play," and its history is largely suburban.

At thirteen years old, our oldest son aged out of the local youth boosters league, which was fairly competitive but

---

[3]"Relax. It's just a Game," Hockey Canada. https://www.youtube.com/watch?v=cq8_DgbJYko
[4]*And the Sun Shines Now*, 185.

still recreational, and the pandemic axed his school's team for the 2020-21 year, so there was only one option left if he wanted to play organized soccer: one of New Orleans' traveling teams. Although school sports had been canceled throughout the city, club teams were still at least training and trying to schedule friendlies or league matches for later in the fall. My wife and I rationalized the $1800 club fee by telling ourselves that the quality of players would help his skills and overall game, and we bought into the "individual player development" that was promised.

At the end of summer 2020, I began watching him train with his new U-14 team. This was no longer the game he used to play at school called "World Cup," where each child gave themselves a famous player's name—Pelé, Messi, Morgan— and then tried to dribble and feint their way through the others to score a goal. No, this was highly competitive play where home and away kits totaled a couple of hundred dollars. I watched players better than our son, a few a lot better. He hadn't hit his adolescent growth spurt as some of the others already had—broad shoulders, moustaches. But he was still skillful, could use both feet, and was a team player, working hard at training, attending each session unlike a few of the more skilled players who skipped sessions. In the first six games, he sat on the bench except for subbing in for five to ten minutes at the end of a half, or in some cases not playing at all.

After a match in which our coach was ejected from the sidelines for screaming at the referee about offside calls, and in the subsequent game later that day, two of our players were red-carded for abusive language, I finally wrote a detailed letter to the club's director. I politely said that we were disappointed with the coaching, especially the lack of positive feedback, and that if our son hadn't been good enough, the club shouldn't have offered him a spot on the team in the first place. There was a long talk one evening as we watched the boys train. The director said he'd not realized how little our son, among others, were playing in games, or how unhappy he was. He would talk to the coach. Things improved over the next three months: the benchwarmers played significantly more minutes in matches, many of them scoring goals, and the group dynamic of the team improved. Kids encouraged each other on the pitch, camaraderie grew. Most importantly, the coach seemed to have undergone an attitude change: crazed shouting from the sidelines all but disappeared, and on many occasions I detected a smile on his face. He looked like he was enjoying himself, even when the team lost.

Then, a day before a match in early spring, there was a note on the team's messaging app: "There will be limited rotation of players during this game and a few other friendly games in spring. This will be similar to how the U-15 NPSL will be played next season which we are still finalizing where substitution rules will be in place to reflect more of a European style soccer academy." I hadn't seen the message, in fact, before the match, but as I watched the six boys on the bench, save for their two minutes of play at the end of the second half, I realized we were back to where we began: winning at the expense of most everything else.[5] There was one problem: we didn't win; we lost 4 to 1. As a coach myself, I recognized why: the boys who played the entire game were exhausted, and the team didn't play cohesively on the field. The dejected faces were not due to losing per se, but to not valuing each other as contributors to the game.

I went back and read the pre-game message, which included: "The U-15 NPLS league will be another significant milestone for the boys as the academy develops players to feed to the U-19 and senior men's teams. This will provide significant exposure for players at a regional and national level as they continue their soccer journeys." "Soccer journeys" sounded nice, but I found myself questioning the entire premise. What exactly is the aim of the academy, to turn out a few players who may someday play Division I college soccer, or break into the pros? Is that what each of the boys should aim for? The day after the loss, another message went out about "every player needing to step up and take responsibility." I had a hard time understanding how this was going to happen with one-third of the team not playing.

---

[5] I once saw a t-shirt on a teenage footballer that read *The person that said winning isn't everything, never won anything.—Mia Hamm*. I admire Mia Hamm, but I can't admire that sentiment. It reminds me of another very "American" idea: *Always strive for more*. A phrase that recently appeared on lamppost banners on the campus where I teach. I understand the idea of working hard, but why must everything be about "more"?

I also thought of what Arsène Wenger said a few months earlier about football: "We live in a society where only the winner gets credit, and everyone else feels useless. But real life is not like that."[6] The first sentence seems accurate, sadly. But the second one doesn't compute: real life is often precisely like that; there are winners and losers, and there are no ambiguities.

There are, however, other kinds of football that don't have to be played like the rest of "society." In December and January, the local boosters organized its first "winter league." Our son's club team had a mid-season hiatus at the same time, so we enrolled him and his sister (her first time ever playing) in the six-week program. Because the numbers were lower (about 50 kids as compared to two or three hundred regularly), boys and girls played together. There were practices and weekly matches, but no tournament or standings. The head of booster soccer was happily surprised by the turnout, and as we watched one of the last matches, told me this: "The boys and girls are learning to understand each other in a way they haven't before. It's fascinating. I wish I could just get a bunch of pizzas and sodas—and beer for the adults—and have them socialize after the games." The ongoing pandemic wouldn't allow any post-

---

[6]Rory Smith, "Arsène Wenger and the Gift of Time," *The New York Times*, November 13, 2020. https://www.nytimes.com/2020/11/13/sports/soccer/arsene-wenger-usmnt-uswnt.html

game gathering, but he was right: we watched kids of various skill-levels, ages, races, and gender/sexual-orientations (there were queer kids, and at least two kids gender transitioning) all play and work together. They were all contributors. It wasn't utopian, but it was a far cry from my formative experience.

Despite worldwide growth of European-style academies and youth clubs, such "different" play is not necessarily a one-off. In the UK, for example, Paul Cooper who co-founded Give Us Back our Game in 2006, and now leads the National Children's Football Alliance, spearheads efforts at "protecting childhood through play." Play here is termed "free play": a type of grassroots football that is not coached by parents or adults and that is free of fees. Children organize the matches where there are no referees, no subs, and teams are picked by the kids themselves—like on the playground. If play gets unbalanced, most often sides re-organize to keep it competitive. But the game is more about involvement than winning. As Adrian Tempany writes of Cooper:

[He] didn't put fun at the heart of his football coaching for sentimental reasons: he is adamant that it underpins the success of footballers in their development, and into adulthood . . . "People just don't get the connection between kids having fun and kids staying in football and succeeding."[7]

---

[7] Adrian Tempany, *And the Sun Shines Now*, 187.

This all sounds suspiciously like what my pickup games enable. And after a year of playing more than 150 three-touch matches, I am convinced more than ever that winning isn't not only everything, it's not the reason to play. As well, losing is not something to be avoided; we will all lose. There are many times, in fact, that I would rather lose than win and have to sympathize with those who lost.

24 ASSESSMENT

At the end of a year's worth of deep-diving into the sport, watching umpteen professional matches and how-to videos, and reading stacks of articles and books, one would expect to know more about the game of football. I suppose I do.

I suppose, too, I could mention how shin guards were invented by Sam Weller Widdowson, a Victorian footballer who modified the pads he used for cricket, or how Thomas Gronnemark, a Danish coach specializing in throw-ins, helps top-tier teams create set plays from throw-ins like those of in-bounds plays in basketball, or how striker Adama Traore slathers his arms in baby oil to prevent the grasp of defenders, or how Josep Colomer, a Spanish scout, fueled by Qatari money travelled across Africa in search of the next "Messi," or how US national security advisor Richard Danzig claimed that one of the best books about understanding terrorists is Bill Buford's memoir about football hooliganism.

Or, I could trace in greater specificity what playing 156 three-touch matches was like for the pandemic players. I have pages of journal entries, including dialogue, about how we had to regularly find new spots to play our little games, either to avoid the scrutiny of park security or because of field conditions (nothing like trying to play in half-meter tall wet grass), or because the sun would not cooperate with our schedule (finding a pitch with lights in our city is no easy task). Such cataloguing would have to detail our myriad twisted knees, groin pulls, hamstring strains, and how "hematoma" became a favorite word.

I could also offer up my own little data as extrapolated from wearing the $200 PLAYR GPS data-tracking sports bra I bought in summer 2020, an article similar to those pros wear to capture body metrics and on-pitch movements. An article that impressed me with visuals like these:

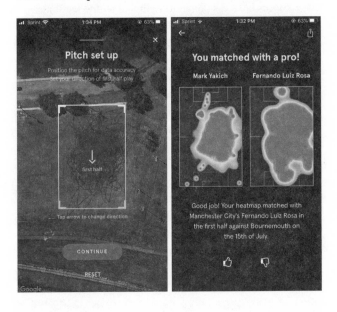

I knew that we covered a lot of distance each match—another player had said we were running about 10 km according to his Fitbit—but I hadn't imagined stats on "top speed," "power plays," "sprint distance," and "load and intensity," or the life-coaching tidbits embedded in the tracker's app.[1] For a while, I went along with the PLAYR's tagline: "Welcome to the Smarter Game." But after wearing the tracker for a few weeks, I realized I was always trying to achieve a new "personal best," amid new and more frequent strains and knocks. Finally, the thing gave me a terrible rash, which I thought might be a virus symptom, and I decided I didn't want to track myself and I certainly didn't want to compete with myself. The bra went to the back of my sock drawer, and I went back to my "dumber" game. The one that couldn't care less about data. The one with no table or standings, which means that after it ends it's virtually forgotten. The one purely its own, like a mandala drawn in the sand, lasting no longer than the time it takes to wash and dry the sweat-soaked pinnies after it ends.

The fact is, some who played pre-pandemic every Sunday have never returned. One, who works on healthcare apps for people with HIV/AIDS, would regularly jog past our pandemic matches, watch for a few minutes, then give us a brief wave and continue on his way. Another, a public health doctor regularly interviewed on the local news, would sometimes wear a sports mask to play. No one admonished

---

[1] Screenshots from PLAYR app, August 2020.

anyone else about their behavior. If there was a lesson, it was that each person had to find their own way through the crisis, balancing what is worth risking, what is not.

We were lucky that this particular virus didn't transmit well outdoors. Between April 2020 to April 2021, roughly 50-60 different footballers took part in at least one of the three-touch games, with a core 10-12 players, including myself, playing in almost every game. To our knowledge, only one of us contracted COVID-19, and that was through a family gathering at Thanksgiving. When the vaccines began arriving in New Orleans, the most exposed and most vulnerable of us got shots. What is now beginning to trouble some of us is that as the pandemic appears to be ending, the frequency of our matches may end too. Players may suddenly do other, longed-for activities. More distressingly, I find myself asking one question: will three-touch be abandoned in favor of "regular" football, what many of us now call "unlimited touches"?

Whether or not pickup games go back to more or less what they used to be, I will never forget the unsolicited "love letter" my wife wrote to me near the end of the first year of the pandemic:

How to explain why after 10 years of resentment over his now thrice weekly soccer playing, I finally came to see it as not just tolerable or okay, but a gift.

It was quite simple, really. Something terrible happened and he was there for me, the something terrible happened to him too, but it happened more to me, and he didn't make it about himself. In the process of our dealing with the something terrible, we grew closer, the pandemic raged on, I worked on myself, and pretty much all of a sudden, those days that he was scheduled to play soccer became a relief to me. Not that he was out of the house (though there was some of that too), but that whatever mood he was in, whatever pain he was in, would be handled, not by me, but by the sheer act of 2 plus hours of soccer. He would come home in a good mood, and I would know that if he went low again, I had only to wait a day or two for the soccer cure.

No mentor or idol could have told me that I could save myself years of frustration and anger if only I could see it that way. I had to figure it out for myself. Today's a no soccer day, but my self-differentiation (my ability to be in my own mood, regardless of his mood) will remain strong because tomorrow is a soccer day.

It's true: when I play everything else goes away. All my worries and concerns, but also all else that I am—husband, father, brother, teacher, bad man, good man, indifferent man. I'm simply a player on the pitch. Which is why I can understand when some say that *football is just football, leave everything else out of it.* They want to take part in an experience that is, for an hour and a half, neither personal in an "individual" sense, nor political in a "public" sense. They want a real escape. And yet, my thinking reverses course in light of what my friend Rodolfo writes about our Sunday morning game:

> Growing up soccer was not really my thing. Now however, whenever I kneel down to put on my cleats and things are weighing me down, by the time I get up everything lightens. Here I am a child again, with a single responsibility—play!
>
> Partly, I play to connect with my fellow players through the language of soccer, where I listen to them better than I ever could otherwise. That is, on the field it seems that I know everyone like there is nothing else to know about them. Yet, I have also realized that I play soccer, come rain or shine, to protest. My protest, and I suspect that it is everyone's in some form—is against our dysfunctional systems. Protest at our capitalistic system and its culture of work that seems to hold a promise of happiness that never takes shape. Protest at the people-technology relationship and at our indifference to the green-and-blue planet . . . and the lack of care for our families with children . . . Protest at the inequality and dehumanization of each other, especially black and brown lives. Playing soccer is one of my ways of saying "No" to horror and suffering.
>
> My fellow players and I have become a community: we care for one another. We believe we're here together for maintaining or restoring physical fitness and for a love for the sport. But I think that below the surface, what

really drives us is the need to form fulfilling relationships linked to the deepest yearning of humanity. It's not that soccer inherently gives us meaning, but collectively and individually we give soccer meaning.

The meaning Rodolfo identifies isn't escapism at all. As SC Freiburg's manager Christian Streich says about the game, "It is part of the basis of life for many . . . As a child, I played soccer more than I ate. It is a cultural artifact. You meet up with a friend, you go to the stadium, you see your friends, you win, you lose, you're sad, you're happy. That's not escapism. It's culture."[2]

What I most appreciate about the culture of the game, including its potential subversion of culture, is a bit of philosophy from Percy M. Young that could equally apply to how I view writing poems: "It is a great thing to be able to take seriously what is unimportant. When we can do this we can begin to take seriously what is important."[3] I'll put it this way: *Football is everything and football is nothing*; the trick is to hold both notions in the mind simultaneously without feeling either one is more "right" than the other.

---

[2]Rory Smith, "The Teachings of the Philosopher of the Black Forest," *The New York Times*, June 13, 2020. https://www.nytimes.com/2020/06/13/sport s/soccer/bundesliga-freiburg-streich.html
[3]*Football: Facts and Fancies, or The Art of Spectatorship* (UK: Dennis Dobson, 1950), 12.

When it comes time to sit down to watch the next match—your child's, a Saturday morning broadcast, or a World Cup game, remember that you see what you want to see. Just be careful of what it is you want. Because if life is returning to a pre-pandemic "normal," we might seriously question what normal really was or should now be. And if you plan to visit New Orleans, send me a note and bring along your cleats. I'll let you know if we're still playing three-touch.

ACKNOWLEDGEMENTS

Thank you to all of the players and friends with whom I've played pickup games over the years in New Orleans—especially those who shared or still share the magic of three-touch. A big hug to Rodolfo Machirica for our "fish beer" debriefs and our close friendship. Thank you to Nathan Henne for his keen commentary on our pickup games, and to Joel Kelly for our shared wonder of Nicolas de Staël. Thank you to my dear friend Chris Schaberg, who co-edits the Object Lessons Series, and who listened eagerly over the phone or via texting to my blathering about the game for an entire year. Thank you to the folks at Bloomsbury, particularly Haaris Naqvi, Ian Bogost, Rachel Moore, Dhanuja Ravi, Zeba Talkhani, and Anahi Molina. Thank you to Sasha Solano-McDaniel who made incredibly helpful suggestions on the initial draft of this book. Thank you to my wife, Annie Goldman, for accommodating and then encouraging my soccer habit, and to our three children, Owen, Samara, and Jonah, for offering us profound lessons on joy and patience throughout the pandemic.

INDEX